Together

With

Montessori

Together

With

Montessori

**The Guide to Help Montessori Teachers,
Assistant Teachers, Resource Teachers,
Administrators & Parents Work in Harmony
to Create Great Schools**

Cam Gordon

Jola Publications
2933 N. 2nd St.
Minneapolis, MN 55411

First edition published 1993.
Second edition published 2001.
Third edition published 2007.

Photographs are taken from the pages of *Public School Montessorian*.
Photographers: Jill Davis, Ann Luce, and Paula Keller.

Book design by Kathleen Timmerman.

Printed in the United States of America.

ISBN 978-1-878373-07-6

WELCOME

MY FIRST EXPERIENCE with Montessori education was as a new assistant thrust into a Montessori environment with little more than a few preconceived notions to guide me. In time I became a Montessori teacher with my own classroom, responsible for the training and supervision of assistants and for working with resource teachers, parents and support staff—all of whom had notions of their own and little, if any, Montessori experience themselves.

I am also a parent. My son and daughter were enrolled in Montessori schools. As parent and teacher I have been part of public and private Montessori school communities struggling to maintain integrity and consistency with administrators and staff from a variety of backgrounds not always familiar with Montessori.

Throughout the past 14 years I have experienced how Montessorians ourselves sometimes create barriers. Too often we keep out our most important allies—parents, administrators, assistants, support staff and resource teachers. Through our special, often isolated, teacher preparation programs and through the Montessori mystique we create we alienate others. Through the richly metaphorical and unique terminology we use and through our preoccupation with the classroom, "Montessori" literature and colleagues, and the children for whom we work, we risk building walls around us and excluding others.

In my roles of assistant, classroom teacher, resource teacher and parent I have felt the need for a tool to help introduce people to Montessori history, philosophy and practice. This book is intended to be such a tool.

I hope that this tool will help you, and others, open the door to the world of Montessori education and break through some of the barriers. It is written for parents and staff in public and private schools throughout North America so that they may better work together for themselves and the children in their schools.

A tool serves no worthy purpose unless it is used well. I recommend that Montessori certified and non-certified personnel both become familiar with this book and that they use it as part of a larger orientation program that includes demonstration of materials, observations in Montessori environments and discussions. I hope that it is used as a reference to find out about areas that interest you, as a background, and as a starting place from which to form questions for your observations, for your colleagues and for future readings. Most importantly, I hope that you use it in a way that works for you.

As you do, be advised that this represents my own interpretation of what I have been exposed to and my own choices about what to emphasize and what to exclude. The choices have been very difficult and I have done my best to base them on accepted and tested Montessori theory and practice. I encourage you to find out what others think. Consult and learn from the Montessorians in your midst. Read the writings of Maria Montessori. Read the works of others as well. I have included references and a list of recommended books to help you get started.

Something or someone has led you to the Montessori educational approach. I hope this is the beginning of a fruitful journey, and that this book will help to keep you on course. Welcome.

> *Not in the service of any political or social creed should the teacher work but in the service of a complete human being able to exercise in freedom a self-disciplined will and judgment, unperverted by prejudice and undistorted by fear.*
>
> Maria Montessori
> **To Educate the Human Potential**

ACKNOWLEDGMENTS

WHAT FOLLOWS IS the result a great deal of reading, listening, watching, discussing and thinking. Many of the ideas and suggestions in these pages are not my own but have filtered through me as part of a rich and rewarding past association with others. I am grateful to the many children, instructors, friends and colleagues I have learned from along the way.

Special acknowledgment goes to Mary Bernard Pabst, who has been a great teacher and valuable resource in terms of lectures, recommended readings and discussions that I have incorporated into this book. Thanks goes to Chule Fernando, Dotti Feldman and David Kahn for helpful comments on an earlier draft; to Betsy Coe for broadening my understanding and encouraging me to make the text more accessible and to Denny Schapiro for his editing skills, creative ideas, gentle encouragement and amazing patience.

Finally, and ultimately, acknowledgment must go to Maria Montessori herself. Her ideas, beliefs, insights and understanding of human development continue to inspire and guide me as they did in the writing of this book.

CONTENTS

1. Historical Background

The Woman and the Movement

Maria Montessori lived from 1870 to 1952. She founded what is known as the "Montessori Method" at the turn of the century and her influence on the fields of psychology and education has continued since. Today, schools and teacher education programs throughout the world are devoted to implementing her ideas about child development and her approach to education.

Montessori was born and raised in Italy. In 1896 she became one of the first, if not the first, woman doctors of medicine in Italy. She was a devoted scientist and insatiable learner. The fact that she was able to break gender barriers is an indication of the courage, perseverance and determination that characterized her life. As Rita Kramer (1976) wrote in her comprehensive biography of Maria Montessori:

> As a young girl Maria Montessori found it possible to bend the rules of her world. She began by breaking the traditional barriers between males and females in education, as she would later break those between teacher and pupil, and in the process redefine the roles of each. She managed her career and her own education with the attitude that change was possible and the conviction that she could affect it. And she brought that general attitude and conviction to bear on the social problems she saw around her.

One of the first social problems that Montessori faced was the plight of disadvantaged children in Italy. During and after medical school she worked with children who had a variety of disorders and were labeled as "feeble minded" and "insane" at the psychiatric clinic in Rome. There she developed and adapted learning materials for these mentally ill and emotionally disturbed children. She published a variety of articles and gave lectures. In 1900 she became director of a program established to prepare other teachers to work with children with special needs.

This period in Montessori's life was filled with intense work and study in the education of special needs children and the training of teachers. From 1900 until 1907 she taught at the University of Rome and carried on a private medical practice.

By age 36, Montessori was a well-known and respected figure in Italy's scientific, academic and socially conscious circles. Rome was in the midst of a period of active social reform. In 1906, Montessori accepted a position offered by the director general of the Roman Association for Good Building to establish and oversee schools and child care centers for the poor families who lived in the tenements the association had constructed. The first such project was in a slum in the San Lorenzo district of Rome. It was here that the first Children's House (Casa dei Bambini) was created.

Although many of Montessori's associates may have viewed this career move as a step down for her, to Montessori it appears to have been a long-awaited chance to work with so-called "normal" children. Montessori used this opportunity to observe children in a naturalistic manner. It was here that her method was started, developed and refined through observation and experimentation. It was in this first Children's House that the Montessori Method was born.

Soon after the first Children's House opened in 1907, more were established in other poor as well as wealthy areas of Rome. News of their great success spread throughout Europe and to the United States. In 1909, Montessori started the first training course for teachers in her method. She wrote **The Method of Scientific Pedagogy Applied to the Education of Young Children in the Casa dei Bambini,** (which later appeared in English as **The Montessori Method**) for this course, which she taught.

Journalists, publishers, professors and social reformers, among others, came from Europe and North America to see the first Children's Houses. They sent back glowing reports. By 1913, Montessori schools with trained teachers were operating in Europe, North America, Australia and Asia.

In 1912, Dorothy Canfield Fisher's book, **A Montessori Mother,** was published in New York, **The Montessori Method** was translated by Anne E. George and published in English and interest in Montessori's work was growing in the United States. One of the first schools in the United States was established in 1912 by Alexander Graham Bell in his home. In 1913, Montessori visited and lectured in the United States. She returned several times and in 1917 opened an observation classroom at the San Francisco World's Fair and offered a training program in California.

Montessori continued to have an influence on educational thought and reform movements in the United States until 1924. After that time, however, the interest in, and application of, her method failed to thrive in this country, although it continued to thrive in Europe and elsewhere.

Three reasons may help explain this.

First, her method lacked acceptance from the academic establishment and was criticized by some leaders in American education. The most notable criticism came from William Heard Kilpatrick (1914) of Columbia University's Teachers College. He condemned the program's lack of provision for social cooperation and imaginative play. In addition Montessori was, after all, an outsider to the mainstream educational establishment. She was a woman, a Catholic and a foreigner—three strikes against her in the predominantly male, Protestant and American-born academic world of the United States.

Second, she was reluctant to relinquish control and trust others to help foster the method she had created. This method was now a business concern from which she received all her income and through which others were eager to profit.

Finally, she apparently lost interest in the United States, or deemed it unfruitful to apply her energies there, and turned her attentions elsewhere.

Kramer wrote:

> [I]n the American experience, Montessori had proved her own worst enemy. Rejecting the interest and support of those who did not consult her at every turn, insisting that the method and the movement were one and the same, and that both were at all times and in all matters under personal control, she insured the purity of the method she had systematized at the price of its place in a larger movement devoted to the principles on which she had based that method.

Throughout the 1920s Montessori taught courses in her method in Europe. Her students during that time included such notable figures in education and psychology as Anna Freud, Jean Piaget and Erik Erikson.

In 1929, she established The Association Montessori Internationale (AMI) to oversee the activities of schools and societies and to supervise the training of teachers all over the world. Montessori was president until her death in 1952, when her son, Mario, took over leadership until his death in 1981. The AMI headquarters were in Berlin until 1935 when they were moved to Amsterdam, where they remain today.

In the 1930s, under the government of Mussolini, Montessori briefly directed the public elementary school system of Italy. This major undertaking must have been exciting for Montessori, who had frequently expressed the desire to implement her system of education on a larger scale. Soon, however, it appears that Mussolini's domination became intolerable. When he insisted that all children dress in the fascist uniform of the military, the schools were closed the next day at Montessori's order. She abandoned the project and moved to India where she taught, established schools for children 3 to 12 years of age and trained teachers during World War II and for several years after.

Throughout the remainder of her life Montessori and her followers continued to refine and expand her method. She traveled widely, lecturing, teaching and receiving honors. She remained the leading spokesperson for her method, saw it as a viable means to improve humanity and was eager to see it extended from birth to the university level. She remained a vigorous advocate for social reform, children's rights and world peace until she died at age 82 on May 6, 1952.

Her method and philosophy of education did not die. In the 1960s the educational climate of the United States once again seemed ready for her ideas. In the 1950s and 1960s Montessori schools slowly began to reappear in cities throughout the country. In 1963, Nancy Rambusch, along with other parents and educators, started the American Montessori Society (AMS), dedicated to adapting the ideas of Montessori for the contemporary American child and overseeing and stimulating the activities of Montessori schools and training centers in the United States. Since then in North America and elsewhere there has been consistent growth in the number of independent and public schools, in free-standing and university-based teacher education centers and in other Montessori societies and associations.

Montessori Today

Today Montessori education is an expanding educational industry. In the last 20 years it has grown into a complex connection of schools, teacher education programs, associations, manufacturers, retailers, consultants and publications.

There are at least nine Montessori organizations dedicated to supporting Montessori teacher preparation programs and/or supporting schools. Others offer publications, workshops or consultations with offices in the United States. In 1995, the Montessori Accreditation Council for Teacher Education was formally recognized by the federal government as a teacher education accrediting organization.

Montessorians from the United States have also traveled to Taiwan, China, Russia, Eastern Europe, Africa and South America offering support to others starting Montessori programs.

Today, there are about 3,500 private and almost 250 public and 50 charter school Montessori programs serving children from birth to age 18 in the United States. There are more than 120 Montessori teacher education centers. Many schools and training centers are affiliated with larger organizations, but others are not. The name "Montessori" is being attached to more and more endeavors.

No one holds exclusive rights to the Montessori name. Programs and products bearing the Montessori name vary widely in quality and methodology and some have little, if any, connection to her ideas.

In recent years Montessori public schools, as well as Head Start programs, have become more common in the United States. While the majority of Montessori schools still primarily serve 2–6 year-olds, programs for infants, toddlers, elementary-aged children and adolescents are becoming more common.

Montessori's influence can be seen not only in the number of schools that bear her name, but in the fields of child care, education and child development. Many Montessori practitioners are moving away from Montessori settings and using the ideas and practices of Montessori education in other settings. Many of her ideas are now part of our common knowledge, language and thinking about children. Other ideas are being re-introduced as part of larger efforts to reform contemporary education.

Among the ideas she pioneered that are now being championed by public and private schools are these:

- "Hands-on learning" and manipulatives, particularly for math instruction

- Structured learning environments designed to facilitate self-directed learning

- Intrinsic motivation and student choice of activities
- Multi-age groupings
- Peer tutoring and cooperative learning
- Self-correcting materials
- Ecological studies
- Global education
- Peace education
- Mastery or outcome-based learning rather than strict curriculum outlines or credit hours.

Over her lifetime Montessori developed and articulated a rich, holistic philosophy of human development and a detailed methodology for its implementation. For more than 90 years her ideas and practices have been used successfully across cultures and economic classes throughout the world. Contemporary research continues to validate many of her ideas. While we remain a long way from fully realizing the new humanity she envisioned, the influence of her ideas continues to grow.

▲ ■ ● ■ ▲

Suggestions for Further Activity

Reflect

- What ideas and conceptions did you have about Montessori before starting this book?
- What had you heard about the Montessori Method and the Montessori *movement*? Do you think that it is accurate to make a distinction between these two things?
- How do you think that the historical context of Maria Montessori's life may have influenced her approach to education?

Observe

- What attitudes about Montessori education do you notice in those with whom you work?
- What kinds of attitudes do you perceive in the public at large?
- How do people respond when you tell them that you work in, or have children enrolled in, a Montessori school?

Inquire

- Ask a few of the Montessori teachers in your setting how they became interested in Montessori education.
- What Montessori teacher preparation institution or program(s) did they attend?
- To what Montessori organizations or societies, if any, do they belong? Why?

Research

- What Montessori schools operate in your area? What ages do they serve? How long have they been in operation? Are they affiliated with a larger Montessori organization? Which one(s)?
- How many Montessori organizations are there? What are some of their differences and similarities? What is the origin of each? What are their purposes?

Imagine

- What if Montessori returned to see the state of civilization and the Earth today? What do you suppose she might think?
- What if the method Montessori started did not bear her name?

2. THE METHOD

A Framework for Understanding

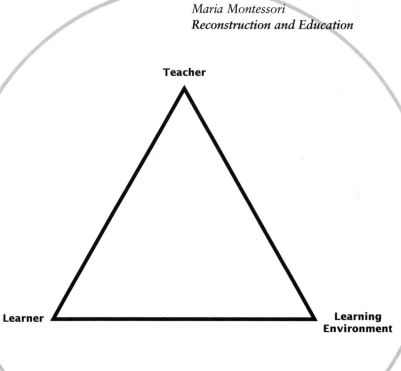

We cannot with our efforts create a man. That is the task of the child himself and it is the most important side of the whole education question...
Maria Montessori
Reconstruction and Education

Teacher

Learner

Learning
Environment

Scientific observation then has established that education is not what the teacher gives; education is a natural process spontaneously carried out by the human individual, and is acquired not by listening to words but by experiences upon the environment. The task of the teacher becomes that of preparing a series of motives of cultural activity, spread over a specially prepared environment, and then refraining from obstructive interference. Human teachers can only help the great work that is being done, as servants help the master. Doing so, they will be witnesses to the unfolding of the human soul and to the rising of a New Man who will not be the victim of events, but will have the clarity of vision to direct and shape the future of human society.

Maria Montessori
Education for a New World

MONTESSORI EDUCATION IS both art and science.

It was Montessori's aim to create a new science of teaching based on natural development, which would enable each person's full potential to be realized.

She designed a system through a process of observation and experimentation and considered these the means to implement and perfect that system. The teacher observes to determine the student's needs—needs that the learner instinctively knows and expresses—and then experiments to create an environment that will allow that learner to meet those needs and follow his or her natural development. All her methods and ideas are based on, and depend on, an on-going process of observation and experimentation.

To a Montessorian, education is viewed as an aid to life. Its purpose includes, but goes beyond, the acquisition of basic skills and knowledge. While students are encouraged to become thoughtful readers, clear writers, skillful computers, problem solvers and logical thinkers, they are also encouraged to fully develop their potential—physical, emotional, social, moral and spiritual as well as intellectual.

Unlike most other educational models, the Montessori Method recognizes the importance of character development and spirituality in human growth.

One of the most profound features of Montessori's approach to human development is its willingness not only to acknowledge the spiritual, but to use it; not only to tolerate it, but to honor it. In this way education becomes a great journey of self-realization and self-awareness as each individual endeavors to find his or her unique place in the world and in the Universe.

While many Montessorians may choose not to emphasize this spiritual aspect, an understanding of it is central to Montessori's approach. Those who emphasize it are usually careful to distinguish it from any formal religious connotations.

Montessori's writings frequently refer to the spiritual development of both teachers and students. Her rich use of metaphorical language to describe the educational process, her focus on spiritual awareness and the role of intuition in her approach, reveal a balance in the method between empirical science and intuitive art.

For schools to be most successful they must be places of self-discovery where individuals learn how to learn and are provided the means and freedom to become lifelong learners and develop their whole selves to reach their potentials.

Montessori viewed education as a means to improve society as well as individuals. She viewed a reformed educational system as vital to promoting peace and improving society.

For the purposes of this book, and to begin to fully understand the Montessori Method of education, it is helpful to think of it in terms of a triad composed of:

- the learner

- the learning environment

- the teacher.

These three elements function together. Learning occurs through the learner's interaction with the learning environment. The teacher is both a part of that environment and a dynamic link between it and the learner.

By examining the learner, the environment and the teacher separately I will describe:

- basic Montessori philosophy

- characteristics of Montessori classrooms and curriculum

- practical implications for adults who work in Montessori schools.

If our soul is far from the child, then we see only a small body, just as we see the star in the sky as a little shining point when in reality it is an immensity of heat and light. The art of spiritually approaching the child, from whom we are too far, is a secret that can establish human brotherhood; it is a divine art that will lead to the peace of humankind.

Maria Montessori
Gandhi and the Child

3. THE LEARNER

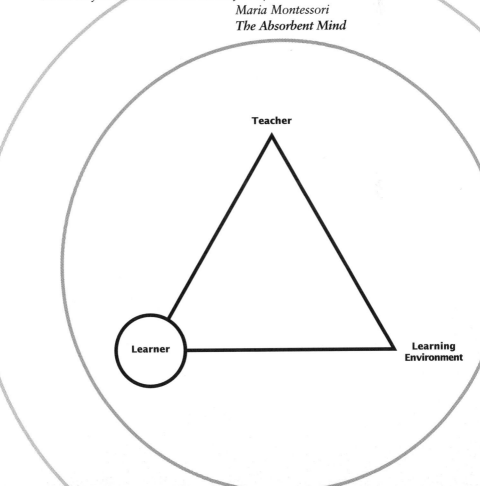

Let us start with one very simple reflection: the child unlike the adult is not on his way to death. He is on his way to life.

Maria Montessori
The Absorbent Mind

Teacher

Learner

Learning
Environment

Growth is not merely a harmonious increase in size, but a transformation. Man is a sculptor of himself, urged by a mysterious inner force to the attainment of an ideal determined form. Growth may be defined as a seeking after perfection, given by an impulse of life.

Maria Montessori
To Educate the Human Potential

MONTESSORI BASED HER philosophy and method on a deep understanding of and respect for children.

She wrote that all human beings are born with certain universal and certain unique potentials. All people enter the world with a unique inner plan that directs and drives them to develop, to master and to perfect themselves. Human beings begin life with internal timetables and patterns already established for growth, both physically and psychologically. If free to grow in healthy surroundings under suitable conditions, children naturally grow into intelligent, competent and responsible adults. It is the task of adults to provide such conditions and aid children in their great quests to develop to their full potentials.

According to Montessori theory, children are living in a process of self-realization and discovery. While Montessorians assume that all people possess many of the same basic traits, tendencies and needs and that they pass through the same basic stages, they also emphasize that each person is different and must be regarded and respected as a unique individual born with the right to live in a healthy world.

The child is a worker and a producer. Although he cannot share in the work of adults, he has his own difficult and important task to perform—that of producing a man....But this tiny child eventually grows into an adult and if the latter's intelligence has become enriched through his psychic conquests and become resplendent with a spiritual light, this is due to the child that he once was.

Maria Montessori
The Secret of Childhood

Four Planes of Development

Our method has been based on the fact that we have been guided by the manifestations of children at different phases of growth. Each of these may be considered a level or a plane. On each different level of life there are different manifestations....The characteristics of each are so different that the passages from one phase to the other have been described by certain psychologists as "rebirths."

Maria Montessori
The Four Planes of Education

Montessori theory divides human growth into four stages of development that go from birth to maturity. These developmental periods, or levels, have distinct developmental tasks and ideal conditions for learning. They parallel other theorists of human development, but in Montessori's integrated theory the stages are viewed holistically and include the physical, emotional, social, intellectual, moral and spiritual development of the whole person.

While each individual will pass through these phases in unique ways and at different rates, some generalizations can be made about these stages or phases. Each phase lasts approximately six years, and each is divided into two three-year periods. These correspond to Montessori curriculum and multi-age groupings.

I. Early Childhood, 0–6 years of age

This is a period of dramatic growth and transformation. Emphasis is on physical growth and independence, the concrete world and the construction of the self as the center of things in a sensory-motor, factual, protected environment. The young child is capable of taking in great amounts of knowledge through the senses. Learning is predominantly unconscious. The 0–3 year-old tends to be more exploratory and the 3–6 year-old more ordered.

The central question is "What is it?" The overriding desire is to "Let me do it myself!"

II. Childhood, 6–12 years of age

This is a period of relative stability, health and more even growth. Emphasis is on intellectual growth and independence, reasoning, moving from concrete understanding to abstract thinking, imagination, culture, research, understanding right from wrong, good from evil and on seeing the self in relation to peers. Children seek to acquire information and find out about everything. The 6–9 year-old is in a more exploratory and expanding period and the 9–12 year-old is more stable and secure.

The central question is "Why is it?" and the overriding desire is "To know!"

III. Adolescence, 12–18 years of age

This is another period of instability, dramatic growth and transformation. Emphasis is on social and economic growth, independence and interdependence, on abstract reasoning, emotional development and on seeing the self in relation to human society in general. Learning focuses on the larger society, community, relationships, vocation and service to others. Again, as in the other levels, the first half of this period is marked by more turbulence and expansion and the later by more stability.

The central question is "How can I fit in?" The overriding desires are to "Do with others!" and "Let me become myself!"

IV. Maturity, 18–24 years of age

This is another period of stable health and less dramatic growth. Emphasis is on the great potentials and possibilities that life has to offer, discovering one's mission or missions, realizing that culture and education have no bounds and achieving aspirations for the whole of humanity. This corresponds to a time of life planning, postsecondary education and one's first job.

The central questions at this age are, "Why am I here?" and "How far can I go?" The overriding desire is for understanding and integration of the self with others and with the world in general.

> *Growth is not merely a harmonious increase in size, but a transformation. Man is a sculptor of himself, urged by a mysterious inner force to the attainment of an ideal determined form. Growth may be defined as a seeking after perfection given by an impulse of life.*
>
> Maria Montessori
> **To Educate the Human Potential**

Basic Human Tendencies

Just as all human beings share the "constructive rhythm of life" (Grazzini, 1979) as seen in the four planes of development, they also share certain basic tendencies. These tendencies exist within and across the planes and stages of life. They serve to assist natural development and their expression is considered important to the well-being of the individual. Knowledge of these tendencies helps guide many Montessorians in preparation of the learning environment, planning appropriate activities and understanding the needs of students.

> *In order to understand Montessori, we need to understand that it is the tendencies of man that govern his development, and that these tendencies must be realized and catered for, if there is to be any real change in the structure and content of education, with a consequent answer to the problems facing us today.*
>
> Margaret E. Stephenson
> **An Unfolding—the Child from 3 to 6**

Montessorians have distinguished the following 11 basic human tendencies:

- **Exploration:** Humans are naturally curious. They are explorers, experimenters and discoverers. Through such investigation and exploration they learn from what they find.

- **Orientation:** People want to know their relationship to their place in the world and the people and things in it. They compare and contrast themselves with other objects, plants, animals and people to see where they are and how they fit in.

- **Order:** Humans work to make sense of the world. Chaos and confusion are unsettling. They readily find patterns and classification systems in their environments.

- **Communication:** People have a natural inclination to communicate. Across cultures and time periods human beings have always worked to exchange information and share experience.

- **Repetition:** Children as well as adults learn through practice and reach closer to perfection through repeated practice.

- **Exactness:** People adjust, refine and improve. People perceive when things don't fit together and tend to work towards exactness.

- **Activity:** It is through activity that people are able to explore, experience and practice. Active involvement with the environment leads to learning and self-development.

- **Manipulation:** People work with their hands. There is a connection between learning and doing, between the mind and the hand.

- **Work:** Human beings throughout history have shown the ability and willingness to work and strive for survival and improvement. People work in cooperation with others and with their environment.

- **Abstraction and Creativity:** Humans have a natural ability and interest in taking impressions and sensations and expanding and altering them in their minds. Humans are creative. They can imagine that which does not exist and can think beyond the concrete and real.

- **Self-perfection:** Healthy human beings have a natural desire to improve. They find satisfaction in personal growth and tend to work toward their own perfection.

These tendencies are most evident in secure and healthy learners. The student who is insecure, ill or fearful is less eager to engage in many of the activities otherwise inspired by these tendencies. Conversely, secure, healthy and happy students will pursue them with little hesitation and often intense energy.

Intrinsic Motivation

No guide, no teacher can divine the intimate needs of each pupil and the time of maturation necessary to each; but only leave the child free and all this will be revealed to us under the guidance of nature.

Maria Montessori
Spontaneous Activity in Education

It is certainly necessary to centralize the interest of the child, but the usual methods today are not effective to that end. How can the mind of a growing individual continue to be interested if all our teaching be around a particular subject of limited scope?...How can we force the child to be interested when interest can only arise from within? It is only duty and fatigue which can be induced from without, never interest! That point must be clear.

Maria Montessori
To Educate the Human Potential

For the natural tendencies to govern and for the interests and needs of the learner to be found and followed, intrinsic sources of motivation must be valued. Trust must be placed in the learner, for he or she is the only one who can know (although perhaps unconsciously or intuitively) what, when and, often, how something can best be learned. This is facilitated through the provision of emotionally safe and responsive learning environments and opportunities to develop self-awareness.

Montessorians recognize that real motivation comes from within. Coercion through external rewards and punishments is often regarded as unnecessary and detrimental because this robs learners of the pleasure of the natural intrinsic rewards of learning.

In their quest to become all that they can, learners can be highly motivated from within by needs for adaptation, independence, acceptance and knowledge. Healthy learners will be drawn to do what they need to when placed in safe, orderly, healthy and responsive classrooms and guided by caring professionals.

Choices and flexibility are important ingredients in any Montessori classroom or school.

Montessori recognized that the only valid impulse to learning is the self-motivation of the child. Children move themselves toward learning. The directress may prepare the environment, may direct activity, may offer stimulation, but it is the child who learns. If we get this principle across to parents, we have accomplished our task as advisors to the primary educator, who is the parent.

John McNamara
Elementary Education and Parent Education

The Developing Mind

Montessori differentiated several characteristics of the human mind and personality. Four distinct but related aspects of the mind help to describe certain characteristics that develop over time.

To some degree all these capacities operate together regardless of an individual's age. Certain kinds of thinking, however, dominate as people mature. As adults we constantly take in and order information, make judgements about it and put it in a social context.

The absorbent mind

The *absorbent mind* refers to the mind's capacity to take in information and sensations from the world.

Very young children demonstrate an awesome ability to take in sensations from the world around them. They spend a large portion of their first years using their eyes, ears, hands, skin, nose and mouth soaking in their world. In **The Absorbent Mind**, Montessori wrote that "The senses, being explorers of the world, open the way to knowledge." It is this ability to absorb through the senses that accounts for the young child's adaptation to the social group, understanding of the surroundings, acquisition of language and culture and mastery of a variety of skills. For the child from birth to age two or three, this is primarily an unconscious process. The young child is often dominated by unconscious needs to absorb through observation, participation and exploration. Sight, sound, touch, taste, smell and movement become gateways to the world. Stimuli are constantly being taken in with great interest, attention and delight. Consciousness gradually becomes more involved and the child begins to intentionally direct and focus attention. Sensory experience, then, becomes vitally important because it is through it that the intellect develops. The child from birth to age three, and to a lesser degree to age six, relies on the absorbent mind. It is said to be unconscious up to age three and conscious from three to six.

> *The little child of three years old carries within him a heavy chaos....He is like a man who has accumulated an immense quantity of books piled up without any order and who asks himself, "What shall I do with them?"*
> Maria Montessori
> **Spontaneous Activity in Education**

The mathematical mind

The *mathematical mind* refers to the mind's capacity to order the information and impressions taken in.

The natural ability to order sensations (classify, compare, analyze, generalize, synthesize, differentiate, associate, etc.) led Montessori to conclude that the mind is mathematical as well as absorbent. The mathematical powers are rooted in, and not necessarily distinct from, the powers of absorption. Humans of nearly any age create order for themselves. It is especially important for the young mind, which has no established order, to have materials and an environment available that will aid in the development of sound, reality-based, intellectual order. This order can only come from contact with concrete, tangible objects in the real world.

The mathematical mind can be distinguished from mental powers such as imagination, although it serves as a foundation for them.

The reasoning mind

Once information is taken in and organized, human beings have the capacity to find purposes, causes, effects and logical connections. Montessorians call this capacity the reasoning mind. It is the *reasoning mind* that allows us to make judgments from the impressions we gather. This is possible, in part, because the maturing mind is able to make abstractions from experience. This capacity usually begins to be demonstrated most clearly around age six or seven. So elementary students become generalizers, synthesizes, analyzers and evaluators as well as classifiers and organizers.

During the second plane of development, from about six to nine, the reasoning mind tends to grow in importance. Learners in this period want to understand why things are as they are. They focus on fairness and begin asking the big questions: "Where did I come from? Why am I here? What is justice? What is right and wrong?"

This is also the age at which the child's imagination blossoms. It is through the imagination that people are able to consider the possible, grasp the magnitude of the past and see potentials for the future.

The socially conscious mind

The *socially conscious* mind refers to the maturing mind's capacity to put ideas into a social context. Adolescents in particular tend to view things in relation to values and their benefit to the quality of society as a whole and each individual's place in it.

Almost as if in preparation for assuming the role of full adult, students at the secondary level need to discover how to make social decisions. These students are often focused on finding ways to belong and make a difference in their peer groups, families, school and community with an intensity not seen during younger years.

Sensitive Periods for Learning

According to Montessori theory, the learner is guided by inner forces that shape developmental needs. At times learners show strong *sensitivities* which lead them to choose experiences that are most appropriate for their immediate learning needs. Montessori called these times of heightened sensitivity for certain types of activity *sensitive periods*. They are characterized by overpowering, sometimes obsessive, interest in particular types of learning. They may result in intense, prolonged activity and always serve to aid development and adaptation. An example is the sensitive period for language acquisition. During the first few years of life, human beings are specially attuned to attend to and practice speech. During this time learning to talk and understand the talk of others can be intense and delightful work for infants and toddlers. Young children will also pass through sensitive periods for order, for writing and for reading.

Once a skill, or goal, has been achieved, the sensitivity passes. If the time passes without the opportunity of satisfying the sensitivity, however, the interest wanes and it will never again be possible for that child to achieve that goal with the same ease or passion.

> *A child learns to adjust himself and make acquisitions in his sensitive periods. These are like a beam that lights interiorly or a battery that furnishes energy. It is this sensibility which enables a child to come in contact with the external world in a particularly intense manner. At such a time everything is easy; all is life and enthusiasm. Every effort marks an increase in power. Only when the goal has been obtained does fatigue and the weight of indifference come on.*
>
> *When one of these psychic passions is exhausted another area is enkindled. Childhood thus passes from conquest to conquest in a constant rhythm that constitutes its joys and happiness.*
>
> Maria Montessori
> **The Secret of Childhood**

While sensitive periods are most clearly associated with pre-elementary learners, the concept is useful for all educators. By respecting and using special interests and passions for learning in the variety of areas in which they arise, teachers are better able to capitalize on self-motivation in planning and implementing individualized instruction.

Effective Montessori teachers constantly watch for and respond to sensitive periods as they reveal the inner needs of the learner. The structure of the environment, the materials and the planned activities all are designed to capitalize on sensitive periods to make learning as fruitful as possible.

Spontaneous Activity

In the Montessori classroom students learn by doing. Youngsters choose from among a variety of materials or experiences and work alone or in groups at their own pace and as long as needed on particular tasks. It is learner-centered, not teacher-centered nor curriculum-centered.

Montessorians typically provide long, uninterrupted periods of self-directed work time for learners. Through two- to four-hour work sessions, learners develop work habits and powers of concentration and are allowed to reach greater depths of understanding.

Through such activity students adapt to the classroom situation and develop the self-discipline necessary to be successful in school and out. Over the period of a year, and throughout the progression of individuals from level to level in their Montessori education, students typically develop more self-discipline and become more independent. Montessorians generally assume that every child has the capacity to function well in a Montessori classroom; with consideration for others, an eagerness to learn and a healthy desire to improve. Montessorians often speak of a process of normalization in reference to an individual's or a group's developing ability to function well in a learning environment.

Allowing for spontaneous activity also helps teachers detect and capitalize on intrinsic motivation and sensitive periods. Master teachers become adept at stimulating bursts of intense "spontaneous" activity through well-timed presentations, dramatic stories, field trips and particularly striking lessons.

> *There is nothing more difficult for the adult than to know how to appeal to the spontaneous and real activity of the child or adolescent. Only this activity, oriented and constantly stimulated by the teacher, but remaining free in its attempts, its tentative efforts, and even its errors, can lead to intellectual independence.*
>
> Jean Piaget
> **To Understand Is to Invent**

In the normalized Montessori classroom, learners act upon the environment physically as well as socially and this becomes the primary means through which educational goals are achieved—through meaningful, self-initiated work and interactions.

Individual Liberty

The principle of *individual liberty* is at the root of Montessori education. Without liberty the nature of the learner cannot be revealed, observed or aided in its development. It is only through liberty that the learner can act spontaneously, follow inner needs, adapt, find order and develop independence.

The idea of liberty is woven deeply into Montessori's concept of the environment as a natural, scientific laboratory and as a place for the development of discipline. Through liberty, the teacher can observe the learner and plan accordingly. Through liberty learners actively exercise their will power and develop the self-discipline essential to future learning. The most valuable discipline must come from within and, in order for it to come into being, there must be the freedom for it to be practiced.

Liberty does not mean abandonment. Montessorians recognize the importance of external support, structure and order. Structure is provided in the set-up of the physical environment, in the materials made available, in the choices offered, in the ground rules established and in the way people behave.

In **Montessori Today** (1996), Paula Polk Lillard describes four basic freedoms for the elementary learner in what she calls a "Bill of Rights for the elementary classroom." These freedoms easily relate to Montessori students of all ages and include the freedom to:

- act by oneself for oneself

- act without unnecessary help or interruption, to work and to concentrate

- act within limits that are determined by the environment and the group

- construct one's own potential by one's own efforts.

Individual liberty is seen in the freedom of movement, freedom of choice, freedom from interference, freedom to work alone or with others and the freedom not to participate or work. As in any community, these freedoms have limits when they infringe on the rights of others. A constant challenge to the teacher, then, is to discover how to preserve and maximize individual liberty while preserving the rights of all and the welfare of the group.

> *Thus here again liberty, the sole means, will lead to the maximum development of character, intelligence and sentiment; and will give to us, the educators, peace and the possibility of contemplating the miracle of growth.*
> *The principle of liberty is not therefore a principle of abandonment, but rather one which by leading us from illusions to reality will guide us to the most positive and efficacious care of the child.*
>
> Maria Montessori
> **Spontaneous Activity in Education**

> *In our system we obviously have a different concept of discipline. That discipline we are looking for is active. We do not believe that one is disciplined only when one is artificially made silent as a mute and motionless as a paralytic. Such a one is not disciplined but annihilated. The child's liberty should have its limit in the interests of the group to which it belongs.*
>
> Maria Montessori
> **The Discovery of the Child**

Individual Responsibility

Along with the individual liberty and freedom in the Montessori learning environment, there must be individual responsibility.

From the Early Childhood level on, students help take responsibility by helping determine the rules of the classroom. Students also care for the environment by cleaning up their materials, taking care of plants and animals in the classroom and maintaining a clean and safe learning environment.

Elementary students often set personal goals, keep work records or journals, participate in parent-teacher conferences and, in so doing, take greater responsibility for their own education. In many elementary classrooms the learners assume almost total responsibility for cleaning and taking care of the classroom.

Teachers balance liberty and responsibility in the classroom. By carefully expanding freedoms as learners show they are able to handle them, teachers help develop each student's ability to assume increasing individual responsibility.

▲ ■ ● ■ ▲

Suggestions for Further Activity

Reflect

- How do people learn to walk and talk? Whose timetable are they following? Where does the motivation come from?
- Recall your childhood. Try to find that "child inside" from each of Montessori's four planes of development—the infant, the child, the adolescent and the maturing adult.
- Have you ever been so obsessed with learning something that you could hardly pay attention to anything else?

Observe

- Observe a Montessori classroom and see if you can detect how principles of spontaneous activity, sensitive periods for learning or individual liberty are being implemented.
- In a classroom, park or home, relax and observe one child for at least 30 minutes. See if you can notice any of the human tendencies being demonstrated.

Inquire

- Ask people you know about meaningful learning experiences in their lives. Did they work to achieve that learning to please themselves, to please others or to obtain some other reward?
- Were they passively or actively involved in the learning? Were they interacting with people and/or materials?

Research

- Choose another person's theory of human development. For example: Sigmund Freud, Erik Erikson or Jean Piaget. Compare and contrast it with Montessori's four planes of development.
- How might the human tendencies have helped early human civilization and culture develop?

Imagine

- You are intently working on a creative project at home. You are very excited and involved in it. The phone rings and you answer it. It is your supervisor from work. She will be over in five minutes to review the budget figures for the next year. How do you feel?
- You are in a sensitive period for learning something at this time in your life. What is it?

4. THE LEARNING ENVIRONMENT

It is through the environment that the individual is molded and brought to perfection....Since a child is formed by his environment he has need of precise and determined guides and not simply some vague constructive formulae.
Maria Montessori
The Secret of Childhood

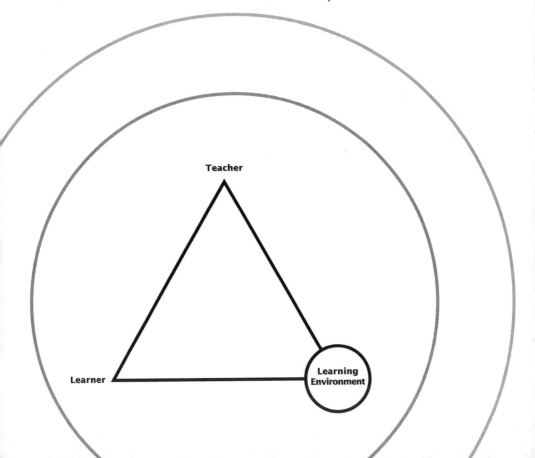

THROUGHOUT HER WRITING, Montessori emphasized the environments in which children live, learn and work. Montessorians see the prepared environment as an essential element in any successful program. It is through control and engineering of the physical properties of the educational setting that the Montessori teacher may have the greatest influence on the student.

The learning environment includes everything and everyone in the educational setting. It is the teacher's goal to create and maintain a physical, social and emotional environment that provides the objects, experiences and all the tools necessary for meaningful activity. It is the teacher's obligation to offer appropriate experiences within a safe, structured environment that will inspire and guide spontaneous activity.

In the classroom, and in the expanded learning environments made available to older children, choices offered appeal to students at particular stages of their development.

During the infant and toddler years the home and the community of the primary care providers make up the learning environment for many children. Some Montessorians have developed programs for infants and parents to attend together.

Montessori wrote that the most fitting place for infants is in close association with significant, primary caretakers and that the infant learns a great deal from being outdoors and in the company of others while with such a caretaker. She wrote in **Education for a New World:**

> *The baby should remain as much as possible with the mother after birth, and the environment must not present obstacles to his adaptation....Happier is the child who goes everywhere with his mother, in streets and market, in trams and buses, listening and looking, storing up impressions of intense interest, and secure all the time in the care of his natural protector.*

Many Montessori schools begin at age 2 1/2 or 3 in the *Children's House.* From that time on, the single classroom constitutes the primary learning environment, with students needing more opportunities to learn out in the community and beyond as they grow older.

All areas used by the learners are part of the learning environment. This includes coat areas, hallways, yards, playgrounds, gardens, gyms and lunch rooms.

Some of a Montessori teacher's most creative, challenging and rewarding moments center on preparation of the environment. This includes arrangement of the furniture, color of the walls and type of flooring as well as the selection, sequencing and placement of learning materials. All these variables, many of which occur long before the students ever set foot in the school, have great effects on what happens when they arrive.

The Classroom

The classroom is the learner's workplace. The furniture, shelves, tables and chairs are suited to the size of the learners. The well-designed environment provides a safe, orderly, inviting place for the student. In the early childhood through the elementary years it is made up primarily of low, open shelves with books and other learning materials organized into curriculum areas and of chairs, tables and/or desks. Often there are tables for individuals and others for small groups. There may also be low tables or platforms suitable for working on while sitting on the floor. Rugs or mats define spaces for children who are working on the floor.

Easels, chalkboards, marker boards, bulletin boards, animals, plants, art work and charts may also be present. The number items displayed on walls and on shelves is limited to avoid unnecessary distractions and to focus attention on the learning materials. Montessorians include only those things that are necessary to assist development and exclude things that are irrelevant.

Many classrooms at the early childhood and elementary levels also have a line taped or painted on the floor. This is used for movement activities and, in some classrooms, serves to define a group meeting space.

Most classrooms also contain a sink, a bathroom (or immediate access to one) and some private cabinet, cubby or locker for each student's personal work and belongings.

Montessorians try to preserve the classroom as the students' work place. Whenever possible they limit "teacher only" areas or things. A teacher's desk, files and cabinets may be nonexistent, in a separate room or pulled off to the side to minimize interference with the student work.

Each environment is unique. Classrooms are prepared and modified as a function of the basic floor plan, the particular preferences of the teacher and the needs, characteristics and ages of the students. The following represent some of the key elements of any prepared environment.

Sequence and order

> *The secret of free development of the child consists, therefore, in organizing for him the means necessary for his internal nourishment....But to ensure the psychical phenomena of growth we must prepare the environment in a definite manner and from this environment offer the child the external means directly necessary for him.*
>
> Maria Montessori
> **Spontaneous Activity in Education**

A sense of order permeates the environment. There is a place for everything and everything is kept in its place. This appeals to the learner's need for order and inspires order in action and thinking.

Organization of the environment facilitates liberty and learning. It is through clear organization that students get an overview of the whole curriculum, can choose appropriate materials and, in a sense, design their own curriculum from what is offered. It also makes it easier for the teacher to direct students to areas from which to choose materials. The sequence of the materials and the order of the environment support free choice, movement and individualized learning.

Order prevails throughout—from an individual set of materials to the separate curriculum areas in the room. Each material or activity isolates some new difficulty, quality or concept within a definite sequence. Materials that teach similar concepts or skills are grouped together and follow left-to-right and top-to-bottom progressions, from easy to difficult, simple to complex and concrete to abstract. Each material leads to future work, building on success followed by success as students progress through the materials.

On a larger scale, the room is divided and balanced into different curriculum areas, each having its own section and internal sequence. There are many variations among Montessori environments, but the principles of sequence and order are major considerations of any teacher.

Self-teaching materials

The materials in the environment facilitate self-teaching, or what is sometimes called auto-education. Each material or set of materials found on a tray, in a basket, in a box, in a folder or in a designated place has with it or at easy access all that is needed to work with it. Each individualized activity is arranged in an orderly way and placed within a larger sequence.

Younger students rely more on concrete, self-contained learning activities, while older ones may use activity cards, their own ideas or teacher suggestions for engaging in research or lengthier projects.

Materials are changed regularly and brought into the environment gradually. The simpler, more concrete exercises are brought in first and prepare for more difficult and complex ones. Activities, or exercises, with concrete materials are demonstrated in slow and precise manners so students see their use. Each has specific objectives, points of interest, standard uses and variations or extensions.

Within each exercise there are controls of error. These built-in features allow students to find and correct their own mistakes. In this way the learner receives immediate feedback which aids successful completion of the task. Sometimes the teacher or other students function as a control of error, but these are exceptions. In general, teachers avoid calling attention to errors. The ideal is to have the students teach themselves through uninterrupted, unjudged activity with the materials.

Controls of error are often simple consequences of actions. When a student sees and feels that one of the knobbed cylinders will not fit into a hole, they see and feel their error. This frees the teacher to observe, take notes and present materials to individuals or small groups while other students are engaged in self-teaching activity.

Rewards and punishments are generally not necessary and are not used. A sense of personal satisfaction at successfully finding the answer to a question, solving a problem, learning a skill or understanding a concept is a much more powerful motivator than an external reward or the fear of punishment.

Teachers may take on the roles of coach and advisor during activities and experiences, especially during the elementary and adolescent years, to help students improve and succeed in their efforts. Still, as much as possible, without risking excessive failure or frustration, the learner is left free to discover, to ask for help before it is offered and to correct errors as they become important to him or her. When teachers do observe errors or mistakes, rather than point them out and potentially demean student work, these errors are noted and used to help plan for future lessons.

> *The desire of the child is to attain an end which he knows leads him to correct himself. It is not the teacher who makes him notice his mistake and shows him how to correct it, but it is a complex work of the child's own intelligence which leads him to such a result.*
>
> Maria Montessori
> **Dr. Montessori's Own Handbook**

Space to move and room to grow

> *Mind and movement are two parts of a single cycle, and movement is the superior expression....It is essential for our new education that mental development be connected with movement and dependent on it.*
>
> Maria Montessori
> **Education for a New World**

In the Montessori classroom physical activity and movement is closely linked to intellectual activity and learning. Both small and large kinds of movement are part of the Montessori classroom experience. Montessori repeatedly wrote about the unhealthy nature of expecting, or demanding, that students sit still or remain passive at school. In the day-to-day functioning of a Montessori school abundant opportunities for movement are provided in the classroom as well as outdoors or in a gym.

The ideal Montessori classroom will likely be larger than many traditional classrooms. The classroom includes quiet, out-of-the-way places that encourage quiet time and less movement, as well as more open areas that allow for more movement. The room arrangement facilitates and guides movement. Learners have access to a variety of materials and work spaces.

The typical activity consists of a student going to select and gather needed materials, bringing them to an appropriate work space, concentrating on the activity ,which usually involves manipulation of the materials, and returning the materials when finished. Movement becomes a part of each activity.

Experiences are also planned that use movement to introduce or reinforce the concepts being learned. Learners may act out verbs while working on grammar or "become" electrons circling around neutrons and protons for a physics lesson.

Different moods and learning styles indicate different needs for movement and quiet. The design of a Montessori classroom allows for these through careful arrangement of furniture and placement of materials.

As children get older their need for space grows. The home and neighborhood satisfy the very young. The 3–6 year-old thrives in the security of the main classroom, school yard, nature walks and a few field trips. Elementary children need to expand this space. They enjoy working in the hallway and moving to other rooms.

Outings into the community and frequent field trips become regular parts of the 6–12 year-old's school experience.

The secondary-aged learner wants to expand the sphere of activity into the community and society. Richer, lengthier and more meaningful opportunities for interaction outside the classroom and school become essential for a successful program at this level. Adolescent programs typically include school and community internships where students work and learn outside their classrooms, as well as trips and other learning experiences that include overnights and may last for a week or more.

Ground rules

Ground rules are the basic regulations used in the classroom to help maintain a safe learning environment. They are the basic limits on behavior that protect the rights and liberty of each individual and the group. Ground rules promote the internalization of behaviors and values including self-control, consideration for others and a sense of responsibility for oneself and the welfare of the group. They help maintain a safe place in which to live and learn.

When used well, ground rules make life at school easier, make the days run more smoothly, enable students to be more independent and help them develop responsibility. The number of ground rules in a Montessori environment is generally kept to a minimum. Whenever possible students help make ground rules. This is usually done early in the year and then again as needed during class meetings. Ground rules are presented in positive, concise and easily understood ways. Emphasis is on safety, respect for others, respect for the environment and the resulting benefit to all members of the group.

When behavior occurs that threatens the safety of people or property, immediate adult intervention is necessary. There are three basic questions that determine if intervention is needed. Is the behavior:

- Dangerous to the student or others?

- Destructive to the environment or materials?

- Disturbing the activities of others?

Consistency is important. Staff should follow the same ground rules as the students whenever practical. It is helpful to make a list of ground rules as they are introduced and discussed with the group. Adults working with students should not hesitate to confer with each other about rules to be sure that the consequences employed for dangerous, destructive and disturbing behavior are consistent.

In the communal nature of the Montessori environment, where everything is shared and "owned" by everyone, many ground rules emphasize respect for others and acting for the benefit of the group. Here is a list of typical ground rules concerning the use of materials in most Montessori classrooms.

1. The student selects an activity, gathers the necessary materials and takes them to a work space. The child does not work at the shelf. This obstructs others, makes it confusing as to who is using the material and limits the space needed.

2. The learner is free to use the material as long as it is treated with respect.

3. After using a material the student returns it to its place in good condition, ready for the next person to use.

4. Students and teachers restore the environment, clean up spills and messes, put rugs away in proper order, push in chairs etc., after each activity.

Many other common ground rules are established to ensure safety when using special equipment, traveling as a group and staying within supervised areas. If you work in a classroom you should make a special effort to become familiar with:

• the guidance or discipline policy of your school

• the approach to classroom management of your teacher

• the ground rules of your classroom and how they are enforced

• your own feelings about "discipline."

The community of peers

The Montessori classroom provides ample opportunities for social interaction, making friends, developing consideration for others, learning how to cooperate and fostering a sense of interdependence.

In the prepared environment, cooperation and a sense of community are stressed. Individual differences are easily accepted and appreciated while each child is treated and taught as an individual. Students of different ages are together in the same group. Classes typically have mixed ages of 3–6 year-olds, 6–9 year-olds, 9–12 year-olds and 12–15 year-olds. Students are the younger, middle and older-aged child in each grouping and stay with the same group for three years.

Students also move from one age group to another within a school to read with younger students, present material, share information or give performances. These kinds of cross-age teaching help create a sense of family. Everyone contributes and takes responsibility for the functioning and maintenance of the environment. Students are encouraged to collaborate on projects and assist one another. Regular times for large-group activities, community meetings, discussions and activities are provided. Cooperation is emphasized. Students learn how to work together and accept each person as an individual with unique strengths and potentials. While student-initiated competition may be accepted, it is not encouraged. Competition is rarely, if ever, initiated or stressed by adults.

Because of the multi-age grouping, the classroom has a heritage. The older students provide leadership and guidance and act as models for the younger ones. The older students also benefit when they help younger students, by reinforcing previous skills and knowledge, developing self-confidence and getting the satisfaction of knowing they helped others. The mix of ages offers opportunities for a variety of safe, lasting and meaningful friendships.

> *...our method has, moreover, the advantage of being able to draw together children of very different backgrounds.*
>
>   *In the same class there should be found children of three ages: The youngest who are spontaneously interested in the work of the older children and who learn from them and should be assisted by them.*
>
>

Maria Montessori
The Discovery of the Child

The social life of the children is an essential aspect of the Montessori classroom and curriculum. The ups, downs and more complex struggles of relationships are supported and enhanced by specific learning opportunities and adults sensitive to the social needs and development of the students in their care.

Curriculum

Montessorians provide an integrated, holistic curriculum sensitive to the developmental levels of the learners in their care. While the curriculum itself is separated into developmental levels, sequences and subjects (as is done within the classroom itself), skills and content are integrated. Sequences are related. Lessons help orient students to whole topics, topics to whole curriculum areas and different areas to each other.

> *The child should love everything that he learns, for his mental and emotional growths are linked. Whatever is presented to him must be made beautiful and clear, striking his imagination. Once this love has been kindled, all problems confronting the educationalist will disappear.*
>
>

Maria Montessori
To Educate the Human Potential

There are now Montessori programs for children from birth to adolescence. Special Montessori programs for parents and newborns, infants and toddlers have been developed.

Programs at the secondary level are rare, but increasing in number. At the middle-school level (from about age 12–15), Montessori programs are becoming more common.

There is consensus among Montessorians about the major curriculum areas and considerations for the three most common age ranges served in Montessori schools today.

- Children's House/Early Childhood (ages 3–6)

- Elementary (ages 6–12)

- Secondary/Middle School (ages 12–18).

The ages of students at each level may vary from program to program. Many early childhood programs enroll children as young as two years of age. The Elementary level is typically divided into Lower Elementary (sometimes called E1) for 6–9 year-olds and upper elementary (E2) for 9–12 year-olds.

Throughout all levels, most schools incorporate physical education, music, visual arts and foreign languages into their programs in different ways.

Early childhood, 3–6 year-olds

The primary goals of the Early Childhood Montessori program are to:

- develop positive attitudes toward school

- promote self-confidence

- help develop habits of concentration, initiative and persistence

- foster curiosity, inner security and a sense of order

- introduce the child to the joy of learning

- build a framework for future growth.

Five curriculum areas warrant specific comment.

Practical life

This area of the curriculum is designed to invite the young learner to act and work on real-life tasks that foster independence, coordination, order and concentration. It is, in a sense, the gateway to the Montessori curriculum. This is the area where a child may first choose work, be inspired to act and develop the concentration, work habits, skills and control that lay the foundation for work in other areas.

The Practical Life area contains attractively displayed objects familiar to the child, including items commonly seen outside the school that constitute the tasks of daily living like eating, dressing and cleaning. They offer meaningful, nonthreatening modes of activity. Chances for spontaneous activity are increased. The materials are also carefully designed and demonstrated to help teach skills involved in caring for the environment and the self; to encourage responsibility and to promote high self-esteem. Students learn to snap, zip, pour, polish, wash, sweep, clean and scrub. They learn to prepare and serve food, clean up after themselves and care for plants and animals. All the while they develop coordination, work habits, self-control, a sense of community, responsibility and greater independence.

Sensorial

Montessori described the senses as the doorways to the mind and early childhood as a time of special sensitivity for perceptual refinement. Sensory stimulation and manipulation not only aid in the development of maturing sense organs—eyes, ears, nose, tongue and skin—but serve as a starting point for intellectual growth. By helping children to order, compare and classify sensory stimulation, their intellectual development is assisted and future learning is more meaningful and useful.

Montessori developed, and others have since refined, precise materials for each sense and quality of perception.

The basic sensorial exercise isolates a sense and a quality within that sense. The sound cylinders, for example, isolate the auditory sense and the quality of volume or loudness. The sound cylinders are made up of two sets of six identical cylinders which differ only in the volume of sound they make when shaken. In this way the material calls attention to the loudness, or volume, of sound. The sets may be matched, graded from quietest to loudest or both.

The fully equipped Montessori early childhood environment will have materials that call for discrimination of size and dimensions, colors, textures, odors, tastes, weight, temperature, geometric forms, volumes, pitches and more.

These inspire careful observation, focus attention on specific qualities and call for identification of similarities and differences. When using them, students judge, compare, classify and draw conclusions. Frequently the learner is called upon (by the nature and design of the material) to discriminate between very similar objects and order them. The mind is exercised as well as the senses. The student is then better prepared for future learning in math, language, science and making sense of life's experiences and information in general. As Montessori wrote, the materials:

> [D]o not offer to the child the content of the mind, but the order for that content.
>
> Maria Montessori
> **Dr. Montessori's Own Handbook**

Math

A wide range of materials concerned with number concepts, numerals, quantities, counting, introducing the decimal system, basic mathematical operations of addition, subtraction, multiplication, division, as well as fractions, clocks and measurement may be found in the math area. The central purpose of the math materials in the early years is to lay the foundation for later cognitive development and for the gradual transition to abstract thinking. The primary value of early activities in mathematics is found in the way they transform abstract ideas into actions on concrete materials.

Montessori often used to remark "present the child with materialized abstraction." By this she meant "present the idea in a material or concrete form; and always combined with an activity. As the child works for a long time with this material day after day...at his own pace, unperturbed, unhurried, gradually there comes off from the materials the very essence of the operation..." Always the child works the operation first in the concrete until the very essence of the rule becomes absolutely clear to him.

E. M. Standing
Maria Montessori: Her Life and Work

Language arts

Language is a large part of life, not an isolated subject. Language development is a concern of the entire Montessori classroom. Many activities in other areas, as well as with a large group, foster communication skills, vocabulary development and other aspects of the language arts: listening, speaking, reading and writing.

Writing precedes reading as children explore with drawing and forming letters, the sandpaper letters, phonetic or invented spellings and the movable alphabet.

The early childhood language area typically contains a variety of "reading readiness" materials, including materials for phonetic analysis, word attack skills and beginning reading, as well as materials for the refinement of motor control for writing, the composition of words and creative writing. The sandpaper letters and the movable alphabet(s) are the most classic Montessori materials for language learning. Labels, word cards and books, as well as drawing and writing materials, are plentiful. Montessori designed few language materials although she wrote at length about language development.

Unlike the math or sensorial areas, the language area often contains teacher-made materials. It is important for assistants, para-professionals, teachers-in-training and classroom volunteers to explore the materials and work with them to discover how they function and what they have to offer.

Art

Although Montessori did not emphasize an art area or curriculum, it has become an important part of the prepared environment. Art activities help develop many of the same skills as other areas, including concentration, independence, coordination, fine muscle control and sensory discrimination. They offer learners ways to express their feelings, experiences and ideas. The visual arts and creative movement represent some of the earliest experiences of composition. The artist, at whatever age, faces decisions of design, form, balance, intent and execution. Through art, students develop their capacities for creative expression. Furthermore, a stimulating art area affords the opportunity for perceptual-motor activity and manipulation that appears to be vital to neurological and cognitive development.

The art area usually includes sequences for drawing, painting, print-making, collage and sculpture, depending on the space available.

Other areas

Other curriculum areas found in early childhood classrooms usually include the cultural studies areas that constitute the bulk of the elementary curriculum—the cultural subjects of science, history and geography. Music and movement education are also important parts of this and every level. Science and geography areas offer exploration and introductory learning about plants, animals, land forms, continents, cultures, countries, the world and the Universe.

Elementary, 6–12 year-olds

The elementary curriculum builds on the goals and accomplishments of early childhood and offers to the 6–12 year-old the richness of all culture and knowledge of the Universe and human civilization. Efforts are made to present a general overview of history and the Universe to students who are encouraged and helped to research areas of interest in depth and share their findings with their classroom colleagues. Emphasis is placed on social, moral, emotional and academic learning.

While the mathematics and language arts skills are separated to some degree, these are integrated into a whole and used for the acquisition of culture—for learning biology, physics, geography, geology, chemistry, history and humanities.

> *There is no interest for the child in a tangled skein of facts, to be memorized and recited in order....Seeds of interest have first to be sown in the child's mind—easily transplanted if first in the teacher's—and all must be ready for the full answering of his questions when he seeks further knowledge.*
>
> Maria Montessori
> **To Educate the Human Potential**

Cosmic education

Montessori wrote of an ordered Universe. She expressed the view that all life and all things are interconnected and are part of a cosmic plan in which everything is working together towards its own perfection and the perfection of the Universe as a whole. Each species, and ultimately each individual, has a role to play in this interconnected, interdependent web of existence. It is a primary goal of all cultural studies to give 6–12 year-old children a deep emotional, and intellectual, understanding of this cosmic plan and to help them see their place in it.

Montessori literature includes frequent references to Cosmic Education. David Kahn (1988) writes of its beginning:

> *So the beginning of Cosmic Education is literacy, dramatic, poetic, emotional and although scientific fact is basic to the lessons, the program is really philosophical in its intent...the role of the teacher is to tell the story. The role of the child is to find the facts.*

The Montessori teacher shares this philosophy by helping students sense the wholeness of everything, the relationships and interdependence of the parts. The whole is represented in the well-equipped classroom itself with its complete elementary curriculum.

It is through the study of history, from the origin of the Universe to the present—flowing through the early formation of Earth and how it became prepared for life, on to the evolution and study of living things, the coming of humans and the development of human culture and civilization based on the fundamental needs of human beings—that a cosmic education is achieved.

Mario M. Montessori Jr., in **Education for Human Development,** devotes an entire chapter to Cosmic Education. He makes it clear that this approach is not the norm in traditional elementary education, but that it is essential to the Montessori approach:

> *Interest in special detail is never activated without prior interest in the whole. Generally in elementary education one finds an endeavor to teach facts as clearly as possible starting with the most simple and elementary and proceeding to the more complex and abstract. The students find this boring and must force themselves to learn by an act of will. To arouse their interest they must first be shown the interrelationship of things in the world—the different aspects of knowledge that can be studied, how they relate to each other or how they come about.*

He goes on to write that one way to give children a global view is by introducing them to ecological principles. Montessori educators strive to help students see the connections and interdependencies in the world, in nature and in human society.

The Great Lessons

The entire elementary curriculum is presented through five stories, known as the *Great Lessons*, which serve as the context as well as the impetus for further learning and creativity in all subject areas.

These five stories, together with the study of the lessons on the Fundamental Needs of Human Beings, help to present knowledge, history, science and all culture in a holistic, integrated manner.

1. The Story of the Universe presents theories about the beginning of the Universe through the formation of the galaxies, solar systems, the sun and the Earth.

2. The Coming of Life introduces the history of plant and nonhuman animal life on Earth.

3. The Coming of Humans shows the place of humans in the history of the Earth.

4. The Story of Language (or Communication in Signs) helps explore how human beings first used written language.

5. The Story of Numbers shows how humans have progressed through time to use numbers and introduces further study in math.

There is special focus on the role and place of humans in the progress of the Universe and students are invited to consider how they fit in and begin to see the contribution they have to offer the world.

> [W]e want to help the child to realize the part that humanity has played and still has to play....History must be alive and dynamic, awakening enthusiasm, destructive of intellectual egoism and selfish sloth....But history of human achievements is real, a living witness to the greatness of man, and the children can easily be brought to thrill to the knowledge that there are millions of people like themselves, striving mentally and physically to solve the problems of life, and that all contribute to a solution though one may find it.
>
> Maria Montessori
> **To Educate the Human Potential**

Cultural studies

Montessorian teachers, following the lead of Maria Montessori herself, have a broad view of culture. Within it generally falls all human knowledge and more traditional subjects of science, history, humanities and social studies that Montessorians present within a integrated curriculum.

The younger learner is in a sensory period eager to take in and organize impressions of the world. The elementary-aged learner enters a more intellectual time—seeking knowledge.

> Psychologically there is a decided change in personality, and we recognize that nature has made this a period for the acquisition of culture, just as the former was for the absorption of the environment.
>
> Maria Montessori
> **To Educate the Human Potential**

The Great Lessons form the framework for the study of all culture and the inspiration for extensive study and research in geography, botany, zoology, history and social studies. They also help to demonstrate how all people, all life and all things are connected.

These cultural studies make up a major part of the elementary curriculum, and include the study of science, the history of the Earth, civilizations and the arts. In the classroom these are organized under the general curriculum areas of history, zoology, botany and geography (which includes the physical Earth sciences as well as social or political sciences).

The cultural subjects are initially presented in impressionistic and imaginative ways using picture charts and timelines. The Great Lessons, stories and other key experiences strike the imagination and stimulate personal exploration of a variety of subjects. Learners may research details at length and are encouraged to share and apply knowledge. Charts, maps, timelines, experiments, research cards, books and captivating stories as well as field trips and the plants, animals, rocks, soil, weather and materials of the real world, make up the bulk of the learning materials in these areas.

Important parts of the curriculum, incorporated in the cultural studies, in the elementary as well as middle school, include the study and practice of drama, literature, music, chemistry and physics.

Math

The elementary curriculum continues the study of mathematics started in the early childhood classroom. Students are presented with concepts in addition, subtraction, multiplication, division, geometry, measurement, decimal fractions, common fractions and algebra using concrete materials. Through time and use of progressively more abstract materials and procedures, students gradually move from concrete manipulation of materials to abstract manipulation of ideas, memorization and calculation.

The goal is to develop real understanding of geometric and mathematical concepts and operations so that abstraction can be arrived at as part of a natural progression.

Without a doubt it is necessary to reach abstraction, and this is even natural in all areas in the mental development of adolescence, but abstraction is only some sort of trickery and deflection of the mind if it doesn't constitute the crowning stage of a series of previously uninterrupted concrete actions.
Jean Piaget
To Understand Is to Invent

Language arts

While writing, reading, speaking and listening are integrated throughout the curriculum, isolated study in language is encouraged through use of a variety of materials and activities. Students continue to receive instruction in phonetic analysis and the mechanics of decoding while reading for understanding is emphasized. While writing complete pieces of discourse with a purpose is stressed, the study of grammar is also typically introduced at age five or six and continued through the elementary years. This brings to consciousness the rules of language and helps students improve reading and listening comprehension, as well as the ability to express themselves effectively.

The history of language is presented and options for researching early written languages, other alphabets and word origins provide impetus for research and study.

Learners are exposed to a wide variety of literature, poetry and prose. Silent, as well as oral, reading for information and pleasure is stressed.

Writing is a meaningful part of every day and students write progressively more complex research reports, personal journals, poetry and prose for communication, fun and self-expression.

Secondary, 12–18 year-olds

Secondary schools in North America have only recently begun to adopt Montessori's methods and ideas. Montessori recognized adolescence as a unique phase of life that required unique learning environments. Some of the overriding characteristics of Montessori secondary programs currently operating include:

- a small school/classroom community

- interdisciplinary, integrated curriculum

- student community involvement and service projects

- student-operated businesses, work experience and movement towards economic independence

- an emphasis on group learning and social interdependence

- the development of life skills

- attention to affective development, identity and self-esteem

- the need for outdoor experience

- in-depth study in academic areas.

Montessori's clearest conception of secondary education involved speculation about adolescents living in a farm community, called Erdkinder, and operating the farm, a hotel and other businesses. She envisioned students applying their skills and gaining self-awareness in real and meaningful ways, while studying with knowledgeable adults.

Implementation of Montessori-based education at this level remains in its experimental stages. Much is yet to be learned. Several Montessorians are making major strides in this area, especially in creating programs for middle school students (Schaefer 1986, Coe 1988, Gang 1989, Epstein 1989, Rosen 1989, Kahn 1991, Leonard 1991, Gordon 1995).

> *Adolescence is characterized by a state of expectation, by a preference for the works of creation, by a need to fortify self-confidence. The child suddenly becomes hypersensitive to the sharp, humiliating treatment that he has up to now suffered with patient indifference....It is at this age that the "sensitive period" that ought to develop feelings of justice and personal dignity occurs. These feelings are the most noble of characteristics and ought to prepare the man to become a social being. There is considerable transformation....Since there is radical change in the person, there must be a radical change in his education.*
>
> *Success depends on self-confidence, on the awareness of one's own talents and of the many possibilities of their adaptation. The awareness of one's*

own usefulness, the feeling that one can help humanity in various ways, fills the heart with noble confidence, with an almost religious dignity.
Maria Montessori
From Childhood to Adolescence

Montessori's vision of secondary education has yet to be realized. Montessori suggested that the most fundamental component of the prepared adolescent environment should be meaningful work for economic gain. This is nonexistent in many, if not most, traditional programs. In others it is offered only as an enrichment, part-time endeavor. Virtually nowhere is it the core principle around which all study and learning evolves, as was the case in early visions of Montessori adolescent programs.

What is, perhaps, most unique about Montessori's view of adolescent development is that she saw sensitivities emerging that do not mesh with the traditional school. This view has not been disproved nor contradicted by more modern ideas and research.

Many of these sensitivities and basic urges at work in adolescents have already been identified.

They focus on the development of personality. They include: sensitivities for making value judgements, urges to explore emerging sexuality and come to terms with physical changes; sensitivities for fitting in and building meaningful relationships, for discovering how societies function, for distinguishing one's culture from the culture of adults, for identifying guiding principles, for finding and testing emotional, social, physical and intellectual limits, for self-definition and expression, for production, for developing personal dignity and for the formation of empathy and what Montessori called "abstract love."

The consequences for individual and society of not providing the opportunity to satisfy these urges are worth considering.

For Montessorians, the inner forces at work and the obligation to provide for them should dominate. Montessori education is all about trusting learners, relying on them to reveal their basic needs and propensities and setting up environments within which they can act independently. Their self-chosen activity, which leads to continued interest, deep concentration and pleasure is a leading indication of success.

In considering the state of Montessori middle and secondary schools today, the priority may be less on making programs fit the sensitivities, urges and needs of the adolescents and more on having students fit the needs of our schools, our larger economic system and the educational system in general.

There are few pioneering programs that have broken away and built themselves based on the needs of the adolescence over all else.

At least one, The Montessori Farm School located in Huntsburg Ohio, opened in September 2000, is attempting to implement Montessori's vision of a farm-based community as an optimal setting for adolescent development. While serving students 12–15 years of age today, it may one day expand for 15–18 year-olds as well (St. Giermaine 2000).

Without more programs centered around meaningful economic activity and a Montessori Erdkinder model (farm or not), the Montessori model of secondary education cannot be effectively evaluated and developed. Such a model may one day offer learners something that will be of real help to the development of personalities in keeping with Montessori's vision of a new education for a new world.

> *The strongest force at this moment in life is the search for identity. Not the urge to learn predominates, as in the preceding period, but finding the right persons with whom they can identify while looking for their own objectives in life, through a change from being protecting by the family towards wanting to participate in their own right in a larger society of adults. All of these things and many more that take place while they are remodeling their inner and external world mean that they are not the proper students for a traditional school. Consequently, it is not a loss of time if one would offer them instead something that would be of real help for the development of their personality at this very vulnerable and insecure age.*
>
> *Maria Montessori*
> **Erdkinder**

▲ ■ ● ■ ▲

Suggestions for Further Activity

Reflect

- How are you affected by the environment around you?
- What kinds of spaces, colors, sounds, smells and materials make it easier for you to concentrate? Relax? Feel safe?
- How could Montessori's principles of the prepared environment be expanded in nonclassroom settings such as the gym, the home, the lunchroom?

Observe

- Observe a Montessori classroom and determine what the different curriculum areas are. Could you draw a map labeling the areas and the shelves devoted to each? Can you determine where on the shelves the first activities in that area are and what the sequence is?
- Observe the traffic flow and patterns of the classroom. Could you add arrows to your map indicating these patterns?
- Observe how children of different ages interact. What is the role taken by older children?

Inquire

- Ask students in a school and classroom what the rules in that school or classroom are. Ask about the reasons for the rules and the consequences if rules are not followed.
- Ask a staff person how ground rules are enforced.
- Ask a Montessori teacher what he or she considers to be the most important curriculum areas in the classroom, and why.

Research

- What are the guidance, or "discipline," policies and procedures in your school? Are these published? How were they determined? How are the rules communicated to parents, staff and students?
- What are curriculum guidelines of more traditional schools and/or school districts? How do these compare with Montessori principles involved in Cosmic Education?

Imagine

- You are given the task of designing a school, and all the money you could possible want. What would it look like? What would you want to be sure it had? What do you want your team of architects and engineers to consider?

5. THE TEACHER

In the "Children's Houses," the old-time teacher, who wore herself out maintaining discipline of immobility, and who wasted her breath in loud and continual discourse, has disappeared.

For this teacher we have substituted the didactic material, which contains within itself the control of errors and which makes auto-education possible to each child. The teacher has thus become a director of the spontaneous work of the children.

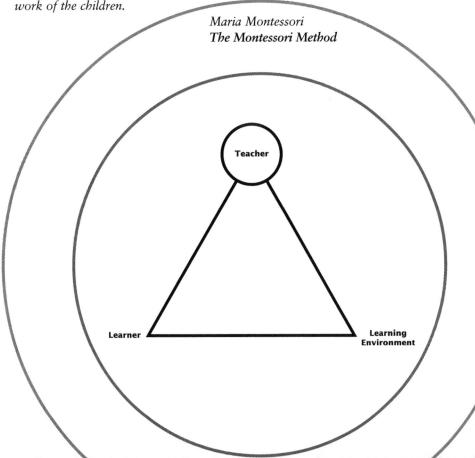

Maria Montessori
The Montessori Method

MONTESSORI ENVISIONED A new kind of teacher. Montessorians often refer to the teacher as guide, directress or director because the teacher does not teach in the traditional sense. It is the learners who teach themselves through activity. It is the teacher's role to direct, stimulate and guide this activity. Through observation, preparation of the environment, presentation of materials, invitations to work and nonintervention when concentrated activity is in progress, the Montessori teacher directs learning and helps learners teach, build and perfect themselves.

The teacher must develop a knowledge of human growth and development. It is the teacher's responsibility to become familiar with current research and a variety of theories about teaching and learning. It is also the teacher's responsibility to be knowledgeable about and interested in the content of the curriculum. A good teacher never stops learning and growing.

> *It is not enough for the teacher to restrict herself to loving and understanding children: she must first love and understand the universe.*
> Maria Montessori
> **1946 London Lectures**

At the elementary level the teacher's understanding of the Universe is especially important. The elementary teacher must prepare an enormous amount of knowledge and acquire familiarity with virtually every subject.

> *The scientific laboratory...where the teacher will be initiated into the "observation of the phenomena of the inner life" should be the school in which free children develop with the help of material designed to bring about development. Then she feels herself, aflame with interest, "seeing" the spiritual phenomena of the child and experiences a serene joy and an insatiable eagerness in observing them. Then she will know that she is "initiated." Then she will begin to become a "teacher."*
> Maria Montessori
> **Spontaneous Activity in Education**

Creator and Caretaker

The teacher is responsible for the creation and maintenance of the environment. This involves the selection, placement and upkeep of everything in the classroom Careful thought and effort are put into the environment's initial preparation and its modification and re-creation every day.

Depending on the janitorial staff available, daily cleaning duties must be done before and after each school day by the staff and/or students in the classroom.

Daily maintenance duties might include:

Before class:

1. Unlock exits and entrances, turn on lights and/or open shades, ventilate room and adjust heating and cooling systems.

2. Check the materials for completeness, cleanliness, accessibility and proper order and place.

3. Replenish supplies—prepare and refill grain and food supplies for practical life exercises; replenish consumable materials such as paper, paste and paint; sharpen pencils.

4. Prepare water exercises—refill water for pouring and washing exercises, dampen sponges that have hardened, supply clean towels and sponges where needed.

5. Make the necessary preparations for snack.

6. Check bathroom facilities.

7. Check first aid supplies.

8. Prepare any new materials, projects or activities.

After class:

1. Refrigerate and put away any food items used.

2. Sanitize food preparation and eating utensils and surfaces.

3. Dispose of dirty water from pouring and washing activities.

4. Sort, file, post or dispose of student paper work (like paintings and collages left out to dry).

5. Clean tables and shelves as needed.

6. Clean trays, brushes and other materials dirtied in the course of the day.

7. Place used towels in appropriate container for laundering.

8. Check bathroom facility and sanitize if necessary.

9. Check materials for completeness, cleanliness, order and placement.

10. Close windows, turn off lights, fans, record players, computers etc.; check the shades and thermostats and lock up.

A specific list of daily maintenance duties should be prepared and posted by students and teaching staff. Dividing tasks and using checklists are also ways to help insure that a safe, sanitary and pleasant environment is maintained.

All people who interact with the learners are also a part of the environment. Give careful consideration to appearance and behavior. Adult appearance, behavior, attitude and mood can have an impact on what happens in the environment. Finding a manner and a "look" that is comfortable and sincere as well as calm, clean, attractive and unobtrusive is likely to have a positive effect on others.

The teacher also must be attractive, pleasing in appearance, tidy and clean, calm and dignified. These are ideals that each can realize in her own way ...the teacher's appearance is the first step to gaining the child's confidence and respect. The teacher should study her own movements to make them as gentle and graceful as possible.

Maria Montessori
The Absorbent Mind

A healthy, well-rested teacher is an asset to any classroom. Patience, tolerance and kindness are important, although difficult, characteristics to maintain in the high-stress profession of teaching. The more teachers can take care of personal needs and stress outside the classroom the better. The greater understanding they have of themselves, and the more their own needs are met, the more they will be able to understand and help meet the needs of others.

Exemplar

Adults constantly serve as models and examples to the youngsters with whom they live and work. Adult behavior has a profound impact in the classroom. It has been said that actions speak louder than words and what people do is probably far more important that what they say. Calm, kind, self-controlled and considerate attitudes and behavior are bound to have positive results. Teachers should constantly try to exhibit the kinds of behavior they expect and desire from students.

In Montessori schools equality of all group members is encouraged. Students are expected to be leaders and active participants in learning and in group decision-making. Through modeling and good examples, values and habits of democracy and respect for others are fostered.

In older elementary and middle school settings the interactions between adults and students can grow and develop into mentorship and apprenticeship relationships. Through these, students learn how to solve problems, complete projects and maintain interpersonal relationships. The adult who has earned the respect of the learner plays an especially important role as model for older students who are working to develop values and a sense of personal identity.

Observer

Careful observation and record keeping are important in planning for individual needs and curriculum. Every Montessori teacher has some way of recording observations and student activity. Older students take increasing responsibility for record keeping and will usually maintain work records or diaries. Clipboards, folders, card files, notebooks and a wide variety of forms and other techniques may be used. Assistants and parents working in the classroom should try to become familiar with the way the teacher keeps records. It is valuable also to practice observation skills, share observations and record them if appropriate.

Observation skills include an awareness of the entire environment. Some teachers refer to this as having eyes in the back of your head. It is especially important, and difficult, in the Montessori setting because a great deal is going on at one time and often the teacher is working with individuals or small groups. To maintain safety, enforce ground rules and insure a healthy atmosphere, a teacher must be aware of all the activity going on, even while focusing attention on one area or student.

Skills of self-observation are also important. It takes a great deal of perceptive self-awareness to see how one's own attitudes and behaviors affect others. As adults, and active members of the learning community, actions and attitudes can have a great effect on the atmosphere of the classroom and the behavior and feelings of others in it.

It is also important to step back, observe and not intervene so that students may practice, discover and solve problems on their own.

In order to develop concentration, independence, self-discipline, and to gain the full benefit from activity with the materials, students must be free to work, struggle and learn without intervention or interruption. This is a basic right in a Montessori classroom. Once an activity has been presented and the student begins concentrated work with it, the teacher steps back and observes. Naturally, harm and extreme frustration should be avoided. Sometimes intervention will be in order. Generally, however, nonintervention is the rule as long as students are working, do not ask for help and are following ground rules. Too often adults intervene, intending to help, but actually robbing students of the joy and benefit of teaching themselves. Usually, through observation, a teacher can offer effective guidance after the involvement and concentrated effort is over.

> *As soon as concentration has begun, act as if the child does not exist.*
> *Maria Montessori*
> **The Absorbent Mind**

Observation is the primary diagnostic tool of the Montessori teacher. Teachers use to it to identify concerns or needs of the learning environment as well as individual students. The materials and how students use them provide daily evaluative information and are useful performance assessment tools.

Effective observation takes practice and open-mindedness on the part of the teacher. Montessori and Montessorians have written at length about the humility and sensitivity necessary to realize how the needs and accomplishments of learners are revealed through observation of their behavior.

> *In the advanced as in the primary stage, the first step to take in order to become a Montessori teacher is to shed omnipotence and to become a joyous observer. If the teacher can really enter into the joy of seeing things, being born and growing under his own eyes, and can clothe himself in the*

garment of humility, many delights are reserved for him that are denied to those who assume infallibility and authority in front of a class.

Maria Montessori
To Educate the Human Potential

Stimulator

To emphasize the importance of internal over external motivation, the teacher is more of a stimulator, a "sower of seeds," than a motivator of students in the traditional sense of the word.

The teacher plays a role in motivation by inspiring it.

The teacher points learners in the right direction and stimulates interest in materials and activities that are likely to meet their needs and satisfy inner sensitivities. In **The Discovery of the Child**, Montessori described the teacher as "the main connecting link between the material, that is the objects, and the child." The teacher helps match learners with objects that will inspire concentrated activity. In **The Absorbent Mind** she wrote that "the teacher must be seductive, she must entice the children."

She [the teacher] must be able to choose an object suitable for a particular child and place it before him in such a way that he understands it and takes a keen interest in it.

Maria Montessori
The Discovery of the Child

To do this, a teacher may quietly and personally invite a student to come and see something special. The teacher exhibits respect and pleasure when using materials. The role of enticer is especially important before powers of concentration develop.

In the elementary years, especially, the teacher takes on a greater role as a stimulator of spontaneous activity.

Through captivating stories, key lessons, bringing resources and living specimens and creatures into the classroom and taking students out into nature and into the community, the teacher works hard to strike the imagination of the learner and ignite self-motivation.

The most effective elementary teachers are relentless in offering stories and ideas from the history of the Earth, civilizations and nature to their students.

Knowledge can best be given when there is an eagerness to learn so this is the period when the seeds of everything can be sown, the child's mind being like a fertile field, ready to receive what will germinate into culture...[A]t six years of age all items of culture are received enthusiastically, and later these seeds will expand and grow.

Maria Montessori
To Educate the Human Potential

Instructor

The main way students are introduced to materials is through careful demonstration, or presentation. In a presentation, the teacher slowly and precisely uses the material in its intended way while a learner or group of learners watch. During such presentations unnecessary words and movements are avoided and actions are broken into discernible steps to increase understanding and the chance for success when the materials are used by the student later.

At times the teacher provides direct instruction. These are typically called lessons. This is especially true in elementary and secondary classrooms. The teacher may give particular lessons to an individual, small group or large group. These range from telling dramatic stories to doing experiments; from presentations of materials or concepts in conjunction with a lecture to active discussions using Socratic questioning.

The teacher also acts as coach and advisor, especially during the elementary and middle school years when learners are much more conscious of their learning. The teacher presents choices and helps students develop objectives, plan future work and review progress.

The decision to do a particular lesson or presentation often results directly from observations and assessments of other work. The teacher may then re-present some materials or exercises to show variations or extensions to help the student learn new information or terminology.

A common technique is called the three-period lesson (also called the three-stage lesson). It may be used with geometric terms or concepts, letter sounds, colors, dimensions, sizes, geographic forms, places, biological information and numerous terms, concepts and phenomena throughout the curriculum.

There are three stages, or periods, that occur in order. They may all occur in one interaction or take several interactions spanning days, weeks, or months, depending on the student and the content of the lesson. If a student is unsuccessful, or uninterested, at any step along the way the lesson may be discontinued and a review of previously presented materials may be planned for another time.

The three periods are:

1. The association of a sense perception with the name, or information. "This is…" The teacher simply presents at least two objects for perception and gives the name of each while presenting it. Students may read the name and content as a first stage. The learner is invited to look at, study or handle each object or phenomenon and repeat its name, content or definition.

2. Recognition of the object or phenomenon, corresponding to the name. "Show me the…" This checks the first period and, through repetition, aids memory. The learner is asked to identify or match the phenomenon from different possibilities with the name or description which the student

hears or reads. The student may hide the object, give it to someone or fetch it from among different choices.

3. Memory of the name corresponding to object. "What is this?" This is the final stage in which the child must identify the object by name. Now the teacher points to the object and asks for the name.

See **The Discovery of the Child** for Montessori's explanation of the three-period lesson.

Supporter

As much as nonintervention, self-teaching and liberty must be stressed, the adult's role as supporter and helper should not be neglected.

When a student needs help and requests it, that help must be there. Part of the role of supporter, however, is found in holding back. At times just being close, or offering a single, helpful word, can help youngsters resolve their own conflicts. Sometimes a gesture, or sigh, or sound, can be enough support. At other times a learner may want and need to be listened to, hugged, or to sit on a lap and be nurtured.

The benefits of a good rapport and positive, open relationship with each student are enormous. Through them adults are better able to assist and share in the struggles, the hard times, the good times and the triumphs of each student. The adults are on the students' side and all students should feel that they can turn to adults in their school for help and support. Teachers should let students know that they appreciate them, that they like them and that they approve of them for the unique people that they are. Encouragement, enjoyment and acknowledgment should all be part of a teacher's rapport. Everyone needs a sense of self-worth and competence as well as acceptance from others and a sense of belonging in the group. It is the teacher's job to help meet those needs.

> [The teacher] must always be calm, always ready to run when she is called to show her love and sympathy. To be always ready, this is all that is required.
>
> Maria Montessori
> **The Child**

Protector and Respecter

Teachers, parents and administrators who work and live with young people share a duty to protect and respect them. Respect for oneself, others, the environment and for life in general are fundamental and essential to the Montessori approach to education. Adults must:

- Protect each learner from physical or psychological danger to health and well-being

- Respect and protect all people's basic right to learn and grow in their unique ways and at their own unique paces

- Respect and protect every learner's right to make mistakes and correct them without adult intervention

- Respect and protect all learners' rights and abilities to take responsibility for their own actions and deal with their own problems

- Respect and protect every learner's right to choose his or her own activity or no activity

- Respect and protect each learner's need to have secure and consistent limits for behavior.

Managing Disruptive, Dangerous and Destructive Behaviors

One of the greatest challenges teachers, assistants, administrators and parents face is the inappropriate behavior of youngsters with whom they share their lives. Reading about and discussing issues of "discipline" and classroom management can help.

Procedures that have worked well for teachers in the past include:

1. Establish genuine, secure, involved and supportive relationships with each learner and a relaxed, comfortable, warm atmosphere in general.

2. Involve children in forming rules, resolving conflicts and solving problems. Use occasions of inappropriate behaviors as opportunities for learning when alternative actions can be discussed and strategies for change explored. Teach problem-solving and conflict-resolution strategies.

3. Model appropriate behaviors.

4. Anticipate problems and redirect youngsters into appropriate activity before a conflict or problem arises.

5. Observe carefully to discover when and why problems occur and how they might be prevented.

6. Be sure the child understands the rules. This may require you to remind the student of a rule in a positive and personal way. If necessary:
   a. Get the learner's attention
   b. State the rule (e.g., "Remember, it's important to stay together.")
   c. State the reason using an "I" message ("I worry that someone will get lost or hurt when we don't stay together.")

    d. Offer a choice ("Do you want to walk back here with me, or would you prefer to go to the front of the group?")

    e. Employ a logical consequence or use a warning if necessary. This is a reminder of a consequence already established and clarified prior to the the situation. ("You won't be able to join us on our next outing if you you cannot follow safety rules and stay with the group.").

(Not all these steps will always be necessary. Often all that will be needed is a reminder or an "I" message.)

    7. Express appreciation when it is sincerely felt and acknowledge effort and appropriate behavior.

After ground rules have been stated and understood, after a student has been encouraged, and reminded of a rule and its rationale in a positive way, there will still be problems with dangerous, destructive, disruptive behaviors. Indeed, students need to know limits in order to feel secure and a structure within which to be free. Youngsters test limits.

When unacceptable behavior occurs and intervention is needed, William Glasser (1969) recommends this four-step sequence of action which is especially appropriate with elementary or secondary youngsters:

    1. "What are you doing?"

    2. "Is that helping you? Your friends? Class? School?" Encourage learners to evaluate the situation and to make some value judgments about the behavior.

    3. "What else could you do that would be better?" Ask the learner to select a better course of action. Choices and alternatives may be suggested by the adult if the learner is having trouble thinking of any. Learners must commit themselves to their choices.

    4. Accept no excuses for not following through and for a commitment not being fulfilled. As Glasser says, "Teachers who care accept no excuses."

Glasser also emphasizes the importance of class meetings for a variety of purposes, including classroom management. Classroom meetings can be used to discuss problems and explore alternatives in a group. Learners and teachers are encouraged to share information and feelings honestly. They do not place blame. Problem-solving and communication skills are also modeled and practiced outside of problem situations.

Most Montessorians employ techniques of classroom management consistent with those of Rudolph Driekurs, as well as with Glasser. In several books, Driekurs discusses the ineffectiveness of rewards and punishments and instead suggests the use of natural and logical consequences. Using classroom meetings as well as logical and natural consequences helps to develop self-discipline and responsibility while also helping to maintain a good learning environment.

Natural consequences allow learners to experience the consequences of their own actions without intervention. Forgetting to bring mittens or gloves to school on a cold day and then suffering the consequent cold hands is an example. Whenever the risk to people or materials involved is minimal, natural consequences can be used.

Logical consequences are arranged when natural consequences cannot be used, or do not exist. Logical consequences have a direct relationship to the act that demands intervention. They are applied calmly and consistently and should have an obvious connection to the behavior that preceded them. To work well they must be applied in a neutral and nonpunitive fashion. The less talk the better. Later the group or individuals may wish to discuss the problem. The more talk or emotion involved during a problem or conflict, however, the more likely a power struggle will diminish the effectiveness of the consequence.

There are many examples of logical consequences. Still, applying them can be challenging. To avoid damaging a learner's self-esteem, always send the message that "you can try again tomorrow." A person who is disrupting the work of others, running through the room or knocking materials down may be given a special table to work at or may stay with the teacher for a period of time. If certain materials cause consistent disruptions they may simply and wordlessly be gone. Consequences usually work better when they are established prior to an incident which calls for their action (e.g., after a student has run away when outside, the incident can be discussed the next day and it can be explained that if the students run away again they may have to miss the next outing for their own safety and the safety of the group).

Teachers and students need to develop a set of logical consequences for particular situations and people. Teachers may have their own ready repertory. At times, instead of immediately employing logical consequences, teachers may choose to use incidents as tools for learning, using discussion to explore alternatives and articulate feelings.

It is important to individualize strategies. The reactionary aspect of dealing with "misbehavior" and using consequences is only a small part of any well-designed approach to classroom management. Find other ways to prevent problems by effectively involving the learner in positive ways, by acknowledging acceptable behavior, by altering the environment and by anticipating problems and stepping in before they erupt.

Young people are struggling to find their places in the group and learning how to thrive socially. Whenever dealing with students in a "disciplinary" situation, self-images and self-esteems are very much involved and very much at risk—beware.

Each and Every Child

Each and every child
has the right to their own uniqueness and
To protection from physical
or psychological harm.

Each and every child
has the right to have clear expectations,
And good reasons for changing
expressed in understandable ways.

Each and every child
has the right to have help finding alternatives
and opportunities to practice them.

Every child has the right
to falter, fumble and fall without intervention.
To support without suffocation.
And to self-responsibility without abandonment.

Each gains from
appreciation of efforts, and celebrations of success
without patronization.

All learn from
authentic communication without domination or shame.
Consistency without rigidity, and
Acknowledgment of feelings and ideas
without probes or invasions.

Each and every child has the right
to be treated with dignity and respect.
And to be accepted, valued and loved
through it all.

▲■●■▲

Suggestions for Further Activity

Reflect

- Recall your favorite teachers. What characteristics did you value in them?
- What is the most difficult role for you to carry out—creator/caretaker, stimulator, instructor, observer, protector/respecter, supporter or exemplar? What is the easiest role?
- What do you like most about working and living with young people?

Observe

- Observe two or three Montessori teachers. Analyze how their behaviors, appearances and attitudes affect what others do and seem to feel.
- At a park, playground, museum or library, carefully observe how adults interact, intervene and behave with children.
- Observe yourself and your own interactions and behaviors in the classroom or setting where you interact with youngsters.

Inquire

- Ask Montessorians what they prefer to be called and how they feel about the different terms for their professional role—teacher, director, directress, facilitator, guide or some other term. Why do they prefer the term they chose?
- Ask teachers what things they do to "take care of" themselves.

Research

- What Montessori teacher education programs are in your geographic area? What kinds of on-going in-service, educational programs do they offer for professionals, parents and others?
- What are the qualifications and job descriptions for teachers and others who work in your school? Are these written down? If possible, review an employee handbook and any other printed material regarding roles and responsibilities of people in your setting.

Imagine

- Imagine the perfect teacher for you at this time in your life, for the things you are currently most interested in learning. What is this person like? What makes this individual so perfect for you now?
- Visualize yourself in your classroom, home or school setting. Take a few minutes and see yourself calmly and competently working, intervening gracefully when needed and holding back and observing when appropriate. See yourself instructing and talking and handling even the most difficult situations successfully and confidently.

6. MAKING THE SCHOOL WORK

The children in our schools are free, but that doesn't mean there is no organization. Organization, in fact, is necessary if the children are to be free to work. It must be even more thorough than in ordinary schools....The school must give the child's spirit space and opportunity for expansion.

Maria Montessori
The Absorbent Mind

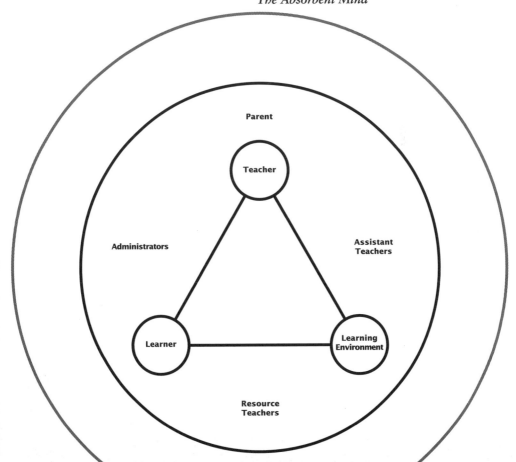

THE DYNAMIC TRIANGLE of learner, teacher and learning environment is at the core of the Montessori approach. For the learner's experience in school to be successful, however, it takes a larger supportive community. It is when the teacher, parent, administrators, resource teachers and assistant teachers work together with a shared vision focused on what is best for each learner, that the Monterssori approach is most successful.

Parents

A child's parents are not his makers but his guardians. They must protect him and have a deep concern for him like one who assumes a sacred trust. For their exalted mission, a child's parents should purify the love that nature has implanted in their hearts and they should strive to understand that this love is the conscious expression of a deeper sentiment that should not be contaminated by self-interest or sloth. Parents should be concerned with the great social question of the day, the struggle to gain recognition of the rights of childhood in the world.

Maria Montessori
The Secret of Childhood

PARENTS ARE PARTNERS in the educational process.

Montessorians view parents as the primary teachers in a child's life. The more Montessori teachers and parents communicate and cooperate, the more the student in the Montessori school is likely to benefit. Many independent and public Montessori schools would never have been started and could not continue without parent initiative and support.

A parent's ultimate role is as advocate for his or her child or children. While the teacher and administrators, in attending to the welfare of an entire class or of a school, deserve support from parents, a parent's primary focus is rightly on his or her child.

Parents may be involved in the school experience of their children in several ways.

Be supportive at home

Being supportive at home can be done best by first being informed. It is advantageous to be aware of basic Montessori philosophy and practices and to use these at home, when appropriate. While it is not appropriate for parents to restructure their home environment into a prepared learning environment the same way it is done at school, steps can be taken to build a child's independence and concentration.

Simple things, like a step stool at a sink or light switch, dishes and eating utensils stored in accessible places and books, toys and art supplies kept in an orderly way on shelves may all help foster independence and purposeful activity.

Providing a suitable place and supplies for study, reading and writing at home will also likely have benefits.

Parents can also examine their own behavior. Many characteristics of a good teacher are also characteristics of good parents. Parents, too, play the roles of care-taker of the environment, exemplar, observer, stimulator, instructor, supporter and protector. Basic techniques of classroom management are easily practiced in the home as well as the school.

Some fundamental things parents can do to support the school experience include:

- Valuing the school experience

- Being involved in the school

- Allowing children the freedom to solve their own problems when possible

- Being ready to help with love and listening when asked.

One of the most important things parents can do is spend time with their children. Reading—both to their youngster and to themselves—provides the clear message that literacy is valued and has been associated by many educators with improved achievement at school.

Maintain appropriate expectations

Montessori education is usually very different from what most adults experienced as children. Montessori classrooms are run differently. Grading systems using letter grades of A to F are rarely used in Montessori schools. Facts and memorization are not given the same emphasis as they may be in more traditional educational meth-ods. Emphasis is on understanding, thinking and problem-solving skills. Correction of work and teacher marking of essays or other papers also receives less attention in many Montessori settings. A student's work is respected and valued and help is given and corrections made when it is requested. It is important that parents under-stand and value the differences between the Montessori approach and other approaches to education and adjust expectations accordingly.

Be a resource to the school

If parents have a skill, a talent, some interesting knowledge, artifacts or a collection of things, they have something of value to their school. Teachers can be asked about how parents can best help. This may involve a classroom presentation or sharing or helping prepare materials or activities for students to use. If parents volunteer in the classroom, it is important that they are aware of how their presence may affect their own child, and of how they then become a part of the professional support staff. If parents assume the role of a classroom assistant or aide, much of the infor-mation in this book will take on greater significance.

Be involved in the larger picture

Involvement in school or district-wide activities shows authentic concern for a child's education and can help a school be more sensitive to the needs of parents and families. Parents must be active in policy decisions and implementation in order for school to be most effective.

Entire schools, or districts, can benefit from an involved effort by concerned parents. Several school districts in the United Sates would have no Montessori programs if it had not been for parents organizing.

Other times parents are able to work together for the integrity of a Montessori program. Meeting together, writing letters and talking to school administrators, school board members and other parents has proven beneficial to many programs. The use of corporal punishment, single-grade classrooms and too much emphasis on "worksheets" or textbooks are all examples of practices inconsistent with basic Montessori philosophy that parents can question and help change.

When a school, or teacher, engages in something that seems inconsistent with accepted Montessori practice it is sometimes up to concerned parents to call attention to it and, if necessary, demand change.

Maintain communication

When written correspondence is sent home it should be read. When parent-teacher conferences are held, participate in them. If a parent feels inclined to initiate communication with a note or a phone call, that inclination is worth following. If parents have questions, they are worth asking. If they have suggestions, they are worth making.

While parents may not be a part of the classic Montessori triad of learner, learning environment and teacher, they do play a fundamental role in their child's school experience. The parent-learner-teacher team makes a second triad and the more it can fit with the teacher-child-learning environment the better.

Parenthood is one of the great joys, challenges and adventures of life. Perhaps the most valuable things parents can do are also some of the most basic and most natural—enjoy our children, appreciate them, listen to them, learn from them and love them.

> *Parenthood is neither the having of children, nor something we do to children. Parenthood is a time when we are pushed to discover the nature of the whole and our oneness with it. It is a time when both our mistaken ideas about who we are and truer ones are brought to light...our children drive us toward this awakening.*
>
> *Polly Berrien Berends*
> **Whole Parent/Whole Child**

Administrators and Policy Makers

Administrators and policy-makers—owners or heads of schools, principals, coordinators, assistant principals, program implementors, superintendents, assistant superintendents, school board members and others—are faced with unique challenges.

Unlike the teacher, whose primary focus must be on the learning environment and classroom community, and unlike the parent, whose primary focus must be on his or her child, the administrator's and policy-maker's focus must be more varied and sometimes more distant. Administrators and policy makers need to see the program from the perspectives of all involved. They must be aware of the history and the goals and mission of the program.

At times the administrator must be an advocate for the teacher or several teachers at the same time. He or she must be supportive and help implement and facilitate teachers' plans and goals.

At other times, it becomes the administrator's role to advocate for the parent. Parents need to be able to turn to administrators who will listen and respond to problems and requests, and represent their views to others, including teachers.

At other times, the administrator must advocate for the students. Individual students and groups of students often require the voice of an administrator.

Finally, it is the administrator's role to advocate for the program both within a school, to staff, parents and students and beyond the school to a school board, owner, other administrators or community members. The administrator can see the needs of the whole program. It is vital that in this role administrators present ideas and accurate information and include others—parents, students and teachers —in making decisions. In this way all those involved can have an investment in and commitment to the program.

Maintaining program integrity is a struggle and challenge, especially in a public setting. Often the needs of Montessori programs are different and hard to understand for those unfamiliar with Montessori theory and practice. Montessori programs do not use textbooks, grade levels, letter grading systems or many elements of traditional education systems.

Teresita Leimer (1991) offers the following suggestions for how administrators, particularly those in public schools, can support Montessori programs.

1. Hire Montessori teachers certified for the level they will teach.

2. Provide adequate funding to equip new classrooms. (Estimates range from $12,000 to $25,000 per classroom.)

3. Group children in appropriate multi-age classes for which the curriculum and method are designed.

4. Let a new program grow with the students starting with a group of 3 year-olds and increasing with one grade level a year adding new students at the lowest level.

5. Limit enrollment beyond the early childhood (3–6) level to those with Montessori experience.

6. Support the hiring of Montessori-trained principals or program coordinators.

7. Acknowledge Montessori teacher training and credit it as professional development towards promotions, "lane changes" and salary increases.

8. Advocate creative ways (like the use of portfolios) of reporting and recording student learning that emphasize mastery learning and reflect the Montessori philosophy and curriculum.

9. Learn about the Montessori Method and topics of relevance to Montessori educators and schools.

Resource Teachers

In the Montessori tradition, the classroom teacher is viewed as a generalist who facilitates learning in all subject areas for each student. At the elementary level, especially, the classroom teacher is an "enlightened generalist" who sows the seeds of culture and offers all academic preparation.

In many schools, especially public schools, specialist teachers are a vital part of the school community and play an important academic role. They offer students experience in music, physical education, art and languages. These specialists, often referred to as resource teachers, also provide classroom teachers with much-needed preparation time. Larger schools usually employ one or more special education teachers. Library or media specialists are also important resource teachers.

Resource teachers may or may not have their own learning environments.

Some resource teachers, most notably special education teachers, frequently come into the classroom to provide special instruction, support and materials. They become part of a teaching team and they should make extra efforts to work in cooperation with the classroom teacher.

Typically, however, specialists have separate learning environments. In many schools these environments are consistent with the organization and orderliness of the Montessori classrooms, except that the materials focus on a particular subject.

In either case, it is essential that resource teachers learn about the Montessori approach and cooperate with classroom teachers to provide students with a consistent, harmonious school-wide environment.

Several areas of cooperation should be considered.

Scheduling

Montessorians place a high premium on uninterrupted work cycles to allow learners the time needed to work in depth and at length. Rather than training learners to follow externally imposed time blocks, students are encouraged to find and follow their own internal work patterns and to develop increasing powers of concentration. Staffs at larger schools go to great lengths to coordinate schedules to allow for long, uninterrupted work times. Some solutions involve making art, music, language, media or gym periods longer, scheduling such specialty subjects only on certain days or back-to-back for specific classrooms.

The whole and the parts

Especially during the elementary years, learners are helped to see how details and parts relate to the whole. Typically, when a new topic or skill is introduced, learners are helped to see how it fits into a larger framework. Resource teachers can build on that foundation by presenting isolated skills in the larger context of meaningful activity for which the skills will be useful, whether it be the mastery of a musical instrument, an artistic product or a physical game or performance.

Isolation of difficulty

Montessori teachers work to divide tasks to the smallest steps to aid mastery. Montessorians often refer to this as the *isolation of difficulty*. Once a learner has an understanding of the larger framework or whole process, the skills and topics must be broken down to be mastered, One difficulty is isolated at a time during demonstration and practice, and each isolated step taught in order. Ample time for repetition and practice helps insure success as further steps are added.

Careful demonstration, using the three-period lesson, providing time for individual exploration, emphasizing respect for each individual, success and cooperation, can all help to make the learner's experience with a specialist more consistent with the entire school experience.

Coordination of curriculum

Resource teachers familiar with the major studies of the Montessori curriculum, who build on that knowledge in their teaching, are enormously valuable to a Montessori program. Art, music, media, physical education or foreign language experiences can be coordinated with classroom-based activities in history, botany, zoology or geography to create a powerful impact on students.

Classroom teachers may also work to find ways to include time and space for students to work on what is introduced during time with a specialist. This may include work with foreign language vocabulary materials, working on art projects, with musical instruments or songs as well as more typical research projects, reading and writing related to music, art, sports or language study.

Coordination of special activities

Learners also benefit from a coordinated effort of all teaching staff towards a common goal. Some schools utilize resource teachers, together with parents and classroom teachers, in annual classroom or school theatrical or musical productions. In this way students apply and integrate knowledge and skills, and become more familiar with each other and more effective participants in the school community.

Individualization

Resource teachers are often expected to work with four or five classes each day. That makes individualization of the curriculum a real challenge.

A first step is to view the classroom, media center or gym as a prepared environment. A teacher can attempt to provide a rich sequence of carefully designed and demonstrated learning materials. Such materials can be rotated and varied according to the topic being studied or simply added to as the year progresses to allow students the option of reviewing and practicing throughout the year.

Peer teaching

In the multi-age grouping of Montessori schools, students function at different levels. Older or more skilled students instruct and coach others. Providing time for small group and individualized, self-directed learning facilitates peer teaching and addresses individual interests, needs and learning styles.

Shared responsibility for students

Resource teachers can offer valuable insights about individuals, group dynamics, curriculum and approaches for classroom teachers, assistants, parents and administrators.

Classroom teachers should include resource teachers in shaping students' Montessori classroom experience by:

- Considering the observations of resource teachers in preparing classroom environments

- Involving resource teachers in student assessments and in conferences with parents and students.

Assistant Teachers

Assistant teachers, aides and other adults often work with students in schools. Sometimes called "para-professionals" or "support staff," these people generally also work with other adults.

Many ideas presented in this book offer guidance for assistants who wish to develop positive relationships with students. The section on the teacher is of particular value to any adult working in a Montessori program.

Assistants and other support staff will also be expected to work effectively with adults. The assistant's ability to work well with parents and supervising teachers can make a significant difference in the overall quality of a Montessori classroom and school. Lack of ability in this area can be detrimental.

Here are some guidelines for maintaining positive relationships with teacher and parents that may help assistants as well as volunteers.

With your supervising teacher

Communication is vital. Be open and accepting of leadership and share your questions, concerns and ideas.

Do:

- Support and carry out direction.

- Inform the teacher of observations regarding children.

- Report information and concerns parents express.

- Report materials or procedures that seem unsafe.

- Ask for clarification and elaboration of rules, practices and philosophy.

- Direct feedback and complaints from parents directly to the teacher.

Do not:

- Alter the environment or curriculum without direction.

- Talk about classroom concerns to any other staff or parents without the knowledge and consent of the teacher. (This excludes violations of law or school policy. If you feel comfortable doing so, bring these violations and your concerns to the teacher's attention. It is also appropriate, and sometimes essential, that these concerns be reported to the teacher's supervisor and/or the appropriate government authorities.)

With parents

Maintain a positive, genuine, open and professional attitude. When talking about a student, focus on direct observation and concentrate on positive things about the student. If appropriate, refer the parents to the classroom teacher.

Do:

- Exchange pleasantries about weather, traffic conditions, news events, etc., in a brief and friendly way.

- Comment on the present condition of the child ("I see Tanya wore her snow suit today." "It looks like Kevin got a little sunburn.")

- Inform parents of something positive their child has done or is doing.

- Inform parents of something previously agreed upon with your teacher.

- Listen to and acknowledge any concerns or information the parents offer and pass that information on to the teacher.

- Refer parents to the head teacher ("You'll have to ask _____ about that." "I can ask _____ about that tomorrow if you like.")

- Respect confidentiality and the privacy of students, parents and staff.

Do not:

- Discuss school or classroom problems without teacher consent.

- Discuss other parents' children.

- Interpret, make judgments on or recommendations about children's behavior.

The relationships that assistants develop will depend on the personalities of those involved. Classroom teams usually schedule weekly meetings. Different teachers will have different ideas about the assistant's role in the classroom. Every aspect of the environment, including the people in it, is ultimately the responsibility of the teacher/director of that environment. The assistant's role is to assist in providing a high-quality environment for learners and a place that parents can feel secure is meeting the needs of their children and helping their sons and daughters grow into happy, healthy adults.

▲ ■ ● ■ ▲

Suggestions for Further Activity

Reflect

- What is your philosophy of classroom management or discipline?
- How is your philosophy different from your parents' approach?
- How do those compare to the approach(es) outlined in this book?

Observe

- Watch the interactions among adults in your setting—between teachers and parents, between administrators and teachers, among staff and among parents.
- Observe different adults helping young people resolve conflicts. How are their interactions similar? How do their approaches differ?

Inquire

- Ask a Montessorian about his or her philosophy of classroom management.
- Ask a teacher about his or her most challenging incidents concerning:
  1. Classroom management/child guidance
  2. Parent-teacher relations
  3. Working with administrators.

Research

- Find and review the most recent school or classroom newsletters, or notices, sent home to parents.
- Find and review the forms, materials and/or procedures used to report student progress to parents and to administrators in your school or district.

Imagine

- Someone has just found out that you work in, or have a child in, a Montessori school and they ask you, "So what is Montessori anyway?" How would you respond?

7. Putting it All Together

The greatest triumph of our educational method should always be this: to bring about the spontaneous progress of the child.

Maria Montessori
The Montessori Method

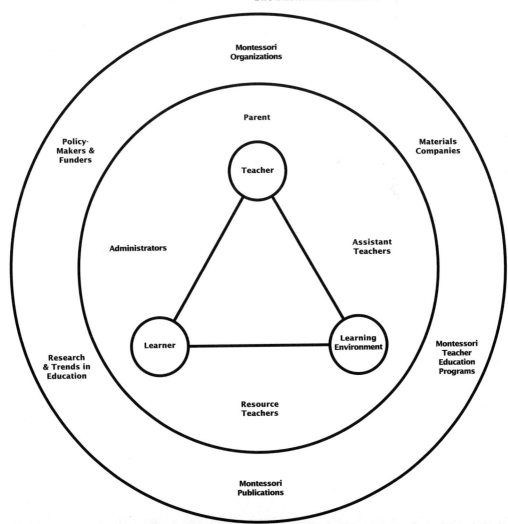

THE SUCCESS OF a Montessori program depends on parents, policy makers, administrators, assistants and teachers working together in harmony. When they do, the positive effect on students can be profound. When they do not, problems are inevitable.

In any school, differences will arise, but it is only through cooperation and the realization that it takes all the parts working together that an effective program can be created and maintained.

Montessori education is made up of a complex web of students, parents, teachers, administration, funding, consultants, other professional leaders, materials companies and teacher preparation programs. Within this web, competition, differences in focus, ideology and personalities are bound to arise. Nevertheless, it is only through cooperation and the acknowledgement of the interdependence of all these parts that Montessori education has survived as a movement and grown as an industry.

Without funding there can be no program. Without parents and students there can be no classrooms. Without quality teachers, effective teacher education programs to serve them and supportive, educated administrators and other staff there can be no school. And without a source of quality materials and an adequate facility even the best of teachers and the most committed parents and students will not have a complete Montessori program.

Montessori education can endure only as long as all these elements work together. Problems with one or the other, or with the relationships among them, account for most of the obstacles and problems faced by Montessori programs today.

Some problems can be anticipated and are unique to Montessori programs, especially in their early years of operation.

Teacher Certification

Usually there is the need, or expectation, that teachers will have additional training beyond that needed for a state teaching license. Many schools require it. There are currently a handful of associations whose primary focus is the oversight and certification of training programs. The oldest and most active of these in the United States are the Association Montessori International/USA and the American Montessori Society. Other organizations concerned with accrediting teacher education programs include the National Center for Montessori Education, the Montessori Institute of America, Montessori Educational Programs International and Montessori Centre Internationale. Many schools require teachers to be certified by a teacher education program associated with one of these groups. There are also a number of independent Montessori teacher preparation programs.

In an effort to create an inclusive accrediting organization, leaders in the field of Montessori teacher preparation formed the Montessori Accreditation Council for Teacher Education (MACTE). It received formal federal recognition in the United States of America in 1995. Through MACTE accreditation, teacher preparation programs gain a degree of legitimacy and credibility. Accreditation is a matter of choice. It is based on a program's willingness and ability to meet certain standards established by MACTE. Lack of accreditation on the part of any teacher education program does not necessarily indicate a lower level of program quality.

Finding teachers with Montessori teacher certification is often cited as a major challenge by groups interested in starting, expanding and maintaining Montessori schools. The time and cost involved in teacher preparation is, likewise, a challenge faced by many individuals who want to become Montessori teachers.

Typically teacher certification programs require additional coursework and tuition for each level. There are separate teacher education programs for infant and toddler (0–3), Early Childhood (3–6), Lower Elementary or Elementary I (6–9), Upper Elementary or Elementary II (9–12), and a few programs for certification at the middle school (12–15) levels.

Additional Montessori teacher education must be planned and budgeted when programs start or expand.

Materials

Setting up a Montessori learning environment often costs more than setting up other types of programs. Montessori schools do not depend on textbooks, workbooks or worksheets that need be reordered every year, but they do depend on quality, durable materials for each classroom to be used and maintained year after year.

The typical start-up cost of $12,000 to $25,000 for a complete set of materials for each classroom creates an additional obstacle for would-be Montessori schools.

Funders must be aware of these additional costs early and understand that on-going expenses may be less if durable materials are purchased early on. Many programs adjust by relying on a less-than-complete set of materials to start and teacher- or parent-made materials. Some Montessorians have argued that the materials are not essential, while others consider a complete set indispensable to an authentic program.

Isolation

Because Montessori education is specialized and relatively rare, parents, students, teachers and administrators may sometimes feel isolated within the broader education system. Parents, students and staff benefit from meaningful links to general education, parenting and professional organizations with people from other kinds of programs, as well as from connections with others in Montessori programs.

Isolation is of particular concern from the teachers' point of view.

Teachers need familiarity with general educational trends and research, but often general conferences, publications and staff development programs seem irrelevant to Montessori teachers searching for like-minded colleagues and education programs geared to fit the Montessori philosophy and approach.

Fortunately, for these individuals, a growing number of Montessori-specific publications and workshops are available. Still, they must be valued by parents, teachers and administrators if they are to be fully utilized. Some schools, districts or local Montessori associations host and develop their own staff development programs or publish their own newsletters to help create resources for Montessori professionals. At other times schools or districts provide time and money for teachers to attend regional or national Montessori conferences. Few things can be as affirming and inspiring as a few days of sharing ideas and concerns with fellow Montessori practitioners from across the state, region, country or the world.

Links to other Montessorians, Montessori organizations and publications help prevent a sense of isolation within the education profession and support on-going professional growth.

Teacher education, appropriate materials and a sense of connection to the larger Montessori community all contribute to the success of a school and the construction of a quality Montessori program.

Montessori Education and Peace

Maria Montessori persistently worked and spoke out for a more peaceful world. Her work for peace was intrinsically linked to her work for the rights of children and for educational reform. Education for peace is likewise intrinsically linked to the Montessori approach to education today.

Living in Europe at the outbreak of World War II undoubtedly made a great impression on her life. In her book, **Peace and Education**, published in 1943 in India, she wrote:

> It is upon peace that the very life of the nation depends, perhaps even the progress or decay of our entire civilization....How strange it is therefore that there exists no science of peace, no science with an outward development comparable at least with the development of the science of war in the matter of armaments and strategy.

Montessori sought to implement a new education for a new world. In **Peace and Education** she also wrote:

> [I]t would be possible by the renewing of education, to produce a better type of man, a [person] endowed with superior characteristics....Herein lies the part that education has to play in the struggle between war and peace.

It is in the everyday life of the classroom, the school and the home that adults are in the best position to promote peace and foster consideration for others. In many small but significant ways, adults play a part in the struggle between war and peace every day. The influence of Montessorians comes through in the general atmosphere they help to create and in the respectful, caring approach they have towards people, learning and life, as well as in more specific interactions.

There are six general ways in which Montessori programs promote peace.

Modeling

Teachers, parents and others help promote peace through their own behavior. Adults provide young people with models of respect, empathy and consideration for others. By being nurturing, significant adults who act with, as well as advocate for, kindness may have the greatest influence in the development of kindness in their students and children.

Perspective taking

The journey from a young, egocentric child into an altruistic, empathic adult is slow and difficult. Many never make it. The ability to see the viewpoints of others may well be a prerequisite to acting with their interests in mind. In Montessori programs, opportunities to know, discuss and act upon the perceptions of others are numerous. In the day-to-day operation of a Montessori school it is difficult not to be brought face to face with the feelings and opinions of others. By sharing differences, learners move closer to understanding the world as others see it.

Conflict resolution

Conflicts arise between people. Resolving them without resorting to aggressive impulses takes skill and learning. Violent resolutions must be avoided. Still, fear, anger and frustration can be acknowledged as acceptable feelings and learners can be helped to find appropriate ways to express and deal with them. Treating incidents of conflict as learning opportunities and viewing social relationships and behavior as parts of practical living is important. By demonstrating, discussing and pointing out alternatives to violence and by being available to help learners develop alternatives, adults lay the foundation for a more peaceful society.

Expressing attitudes

The lives of youth are filled with stories, mythology, current events and personal as well as public incidents that provide opportunities for clarifying values and sharing attitudes. In studying the Story of the Universe, the Needs of Human Beings and geography, history and biology, more opportunities to share values are provided. In the tolerant, democratic nature of a Montessori classroom, attitudes and values are easily and regularly expressed and explored.

Many people are often fascinated with weapons, war history, current military actions, violence and war play. These fascinations can be used to discuss what these things represent. The images, objects and activities included in the learning environment also send messages to learners. Adults can be honest and genuine and share their feelings about violence in play, in the mass media and in the world.

People, young or old, also tend to be helpful, kind, thoughtful and loving. It is important to show appreciation for these attitudes and behaviors from time to time when it is authentically felt. Parents and teachers can respectfully appreciate the value of helpful behaviors without robbing youngsters of the intrinsic rewards such behavior yields.

Creating an atmosphere of cooperation and interdependence

Montessorians emphasize interdependence and a sense of community. They allow learners to have real responsibilities caring for and helping each other, contributing ideas, collaborating on projects and helping make group decisions.

Students of varying ages, abilities and backgrounds are grouped together in the same classroom community. This fosters an acceptance of differences and an expectation that cooperation is necessary. Competition is avoided because the community is viewed as a diverse group of individuals with unique strengths at differing levels of development. The multi-age, multi-ability groups provide abundant opportunities for students to help, teach and work with each other. In doing so they learn how to work with others and how people depend on one another in human communities.

Fostering independence

Helping individuals to be independent, critical thinkers and actors is also essential to peace education. In **Peace and Education** Montessori wrote:

> The child who has never learned to act alone, to direct his own actions, to govern his own will, grows into an adult who is easily led and must always lean on others....The obedience which is expected of the child in both home and school—an obedience admitting neither of reason nor of justice—prepares men to be docile to blind forces....Thus discipline becomes at last a synonym for slavery....For, in reality, the cause of war does not lie in armaments, but in the men who make use of them.

John Bremer (1985) put it this way at a conference entitled Montessori: Peace and Education:

> [A]s long as our society is based on force we can do little to avoid war. We do not expect people—especially children—to do what is right, we expect them to do what they are told, and we easily confuse the two and suppose that what we (or they) are told is right or true.

Montessori education does not aim to develop compliant, obedient learners, but rather to provide, accept and encourage liberty so that students develop the ability and courage to question authority, the wisdom to judge what is right and the independent self-disciplined will that is required to meet the challenges of the future. The challenge of building peaceful, safe selves, families, communities, nations and a world, will not be the least of these.

Montessorians place more emphasis on working for peace through one's approach to life, learning and people, as well as the concept of Cosmic Education, than on any specific subject matter. Learning about current events, other cultures and history all offer avenues worth pursuing in a peace curriculum. Still, rather than focus on a separate curriculum content or attempt to define or teach about peace, it is through the process of living peace in a democratic community of liberty, acceptance, interdependence and cooperation that peace is made an integral part of Montessori education every day.

> *Peace is a goal that can be attained only through common accord, and the means to achieve this peace are twofold: first, an immediate effort to resolve conflicts without recourse to violence—in other words, to prevent war— and second, a long term effort to establish a lasting peace among men. Preventing conflicts is the work of politics; establishing peace is the work of education. We must convince the world of the need for a universal, collective effort to build the foundation for peace.*
>
> Maria Montessori
> **Peace and Education**

▲ ■ ● ■ ▲

Suggestions for Further Activity

Reflect

- If you had to choose only one word or concept to describe the Montessori approach, what would it be and why?
- What two or three things do you find the most appealing or attractive about Montessori education? The most uncomfortable? Why?

Observe

- Sit in on a parent-teacher, or student-teacher-parent, conference and observe the interaction.
- Sit in on a faculty meeting, a parent-teacher-student organization meeting or a classroom team meeting and observe the interactions.

Inquire

- Ask a Montessorian about his or her interactions with other educators. Are Montessori's ideas given a fair hearing? Are Montessori educators looked at differently?
- Ask a college of education professor how he or she view and teaches the Montessori approach.

Research

- How is parent involvement encouraged, and discouraged, in your setting? Is there a policy regarding the role of parents? Are parents included in policy decisions? Are regular communications sent home to parents? How often are conferences arranged? Do parents help in the classroom and school? Does your school offer a formal parent education program?
- How do teachers and adminstrators determine what professional organizations they belong to? What are the most common ones? Does the school provide any help with individual memberships? Is you school affiliated with an organization?
- What Montessori publications are available in your community? In your local library? In your school? Find some and review them.
- How oftern to teachers, adminstrators and parents meet and plan together in your school?
- What kind of relationship, if any, do the Montessori teacher education programs in your area have with your school?

Imagine

- If you could change three things about your school that would make it more consistent with an ideal Montessori program, what would they be?

RECOMMENDED READING

THE FOLLOWING BOOKS offer introductions and overviews of Montessori theory and practice. Standing also includes a biography. Please see the References for more complete bibliographic information.

- Chattin-McNichols, John, **The Montessori Controversy**
- Lillard, Paula Polk, **Montessori, A Modern Approach**
- Lillard, Paula Polk, **Montessori Today**
- Loeffler, Margaret (Ed) **Montessori in Contemporary American Culture**
- Neubert, Ann Burke, **A Way of Learning**
- Rambusch, Nancy, **Learning How to Learn**
- Standing, E M, **Maria Montessori, Her Life and Work.**

This is an excellent, well-researched, biography.
- Kramer, Rita: **Maria Montessori, A Biography**

These are all good books by Maria Montessori.
- **The Montessori Method**
- **The Discovery of the Child**
- **The Secret of Childhood**
- **The Absorbent Mind**
- **Education for a New World**

These are all helpful books regarding guidance and communication, among other things.
- Briggs, Dorothy Corkille, **Your Child's Self-Esteem**
- Driekurs, Rudolph, **Children: The Challenge**
- Driekurs, Rudolph, **Maintaining Sanity in the Classroom**
- Driekurs, Rudolph, and Cassel, Pearl: **Discipline Without Tears**
- Ginott, Hiam, **Between Parent and Child**
- Ginott, Hiam, **Teacher and Child**
- Glasser, William, **Schools Without Failure**

FOR FURTHER INFORMATION ABOUT MONTESSORI EDUCATION

Montessori organizations

American Montessori Society, 281 Park Av. S. 6th Floor, New York NY 10010, (212) 358-1250, www.americanmontessorisociety.org

Association Montessori International/USA, 410 Alexander St., Rochester NY 14607-1028, 585-461-5920, 800-872-2643, www.montessori-ami.org

Center For Public Montessori Programs, 2933 N. 2nd St. Minneapolis MN 55411, (612) 529-5001

Consejo Interamericano Montessori, 416 N. Beringer Cir. Urbana IL 61802, (217) 328-1341, www.cimla.org

International Assn. for Montesori Education, www.iame-montessori.org

International Montessori Council, PO Box 130 Terra Ceia FL 34250-0130, (941) 729-9565, 800-655-5843

Montessori Accreditation Council for Teacher Education Commission, 524 Main St. #202 Racine WI 53403, 262-898-1846, 888-446-2283, www.macte.org

Montessori Educational Programs International, PO Box 2199 Gray GA 31032, (478) 986-2768, www.mepiforum.org

Montessori Europe, http://www.montessori-europe.com

Montessori Institute of America, 23807 98th Av. S. Kent WA 98031, (253-859-2262, 866-856-2262

North American Montessori Teachers' Association, 13693 Butternut Rd. Burton OH 44021, (440) 834-4011, www.montessori-namta.org

Pan American Montessori Society, 752 Red Coat Cove, Kennesaw GA 30152, (678) 797-2160

Montessori publications

American Montessori Consulting Newsletter, a periodic publication on the Internet through the company's web site, www.amonco.org American Montessori Consulting, PO Box 5062. Rossmoor, CA 90720.

El Boletin, newsletter of Consejo Interamericano Montessori, published as a supplement to Public School Montessorian.

M: The Magazine For Montessori Families, a magazine that premiered in January 2006 , published by M: Publications, LLC, 3 Werner Way # 300, Lebanon, NJ 08833, T: 908-849-7880.

MIA Visions, newsletter of the Montessori Institute of America, PO Box 15196, Loves Park, IL 61132, (206) 859-2735.

Montessori Leadership, magazine of the International Montessori Council, 400 Miguel Bay Dr., PO Box 130, Terra Ceia Island, FL 34250-0130 941-729-9565

Montessori Life, magazine of the American Montessori Society, 281 Park Av. S. 6th Floor New York, NY 10011 212 358-1250

Montessori News, newspaper of the International Montessori Society, 8115 Fenton St. #304., Silver Spring, MD 20910, (301) 589-1127.

Montessori Observer, newsletter of the International Montessori Society, 8115 Fenton St. #304, Silver Spring, MD 20910, (301) 589-1127.

Montessori Theory Into Practice, newsletter and job listings of North American Montessori Teachers' Association, 13693 Butternut Rd., Burton, OH 44106, (440) 834-4011.

NAMTA Journal, journal of the North American Montessori Teachers' Association, 13693 Butternut Rd., Burton, OH 44106, (440) 834-4011.

Public School Montessorian, quarterly independent newspaper, Jola Publications, 2933 N. 2nd St., Minneapolis, MN 55411, (612) 529-5001.

Tomorrow's Child, magazine of the Montessori Foundation 400 Miguel Bay Dr., PO Box 130, Terra Ceia Island, FL 34250-0130 941-729-9565 .

Video & DVD

There has been a dramatic increase in information on Montessori education available on video and DVDs in recent years. Here are some primary sources:

Educational Video Publishing
www.edvid.com
North American Montessori Teachers' Association
www.montessori-namta.org
Montessori Foundation
www.montessori-foundation-books.org

AFTERWORD

I HOPE THAT this book has made you more familiar with Maria Montessori and the method of education she founded. If it has helped you feel more confident and know more of what to expect and why, while working in the Montessori environment, it has served its purpose well.

The information in this book represents only a small fraction of all the information, thinking and theories about Montessori education today. It represents the fraction that I believe will be the most useful for someone entering the field of Montessori education, whether as an assistant teacher, parent, resource teacher or administrator. It also represents my own biases, influences and interpretations, which may differ from those of other educators and Montessorians.

So, let this book be a starting point and a reference from which you may continue to develop your understanding of Montessori education and human development. Use it as you continue to work with children and adolescents in your school and with others, and as you turn to other sources in your endeavor to become more knowledgeable and effective.

Our care of the child should be governed, not by the desire to make him learn things but the endeavor always to keep burning within him that light which is called intelligence.

> Maria Montessori
> **Spontaneous Activity in Education**

REFERENCES

Berends, Polly Berrien. **Whole Parent/Whole Child**. New York: Harper and Row, 1983.

Bremer, John. "Education as Peace." **The NAMTA Quarterly**. Vol. 11, No. 1, Fall 1985.

Briggs, Dorothy Corkille. **Your Child's Self-Esteem**. New York: Doubleday & Co., 1970.

Chattin-McNichols, John. **The Montessori Controversy**. New York: Delmar Publishers, 1991.

Coe, Elisabeth J. "Creating a Holistic, Developmentally Responsive Learning Environment that Empowers the Early Adolescent." Unpublished Manuscript. 1988.

Dreikurs, Rudolph, with Stola, Vicki. **Children: The Challenge**. New York: Hawthorne Books Inc., 1964.

Dreikurs, Rudolph and Cassel, Pearl. **Discipline Without Tears**. New York: Hawthorne Books, 1972.

Dreikurs, Rudolph; Grunwald, Bernice and Pepper, Floyd C. **Maintaining Sanity in the Classroom: Illustrated Teaching Techniques**. New York: Harper & Row, 1971.

Epstein, Paul. "Junior High: A Look At Elements of Successful Programs." **Public School Montessorian**. Vol. 1, No. 4, Summer, 1989.

Fisher, Dorothy Canfield. **A Montessori Mother**. New York: Henry Holt & Co., 1912.

Gang, Phil. "An Overview Of Adolescence." **The NAMTA Journal**. Vol. 12, No. 1, Fall-Winter, 1986.

Gang, Phil. **Rethinking Education**. Atlanta: Dagaz Press, 1989.

Ginott, Hiam G. **Between Parent and Child**. New York: Macmillan Co., 1965.

Ginott, Hiam G. **Teacher and Child**. New York: Avon Books, 1972.

Glasser, William. **Schools Without Failure**. New York: Harper & Row, 1969.

Glasser, William. **Control Theory in the Classroom**. New York: Harper & Row, 1986.

Gordon, Cam. "Middle School Pioneers." **Public School Montessorian**. Vol. 7, No. 2, Winter, 1995.

Grazzini, Camillo. "Characteristics of the Child in the Elementary School." **AMI Communications**. Vol. 2, No. 3, Copyright: Montessori-Peirson Estates and AMI, 1973.

Kahn, David. "Cosmic Education: Sowing Life Not Theories." **The NAMTA Journal**. Vol. 13, No. 2, Spring, 82-91, 1988.

Kahn, David. "Experiment for the Experiment." **The NAMTA Journal**. Vol. 16, No. 3, 1991.

Kilpatrick, William Heard. **The Montessori System Examined**. Cambridge, MA: The Riverside Press, 1914.

Kramer, Rita. **Maria Montessori, A Biography**. New York: Capricorn Books, G.P. Putnam's Sons, 1976.

Leimer, Teresita et al. "What Montessori Teachers Would Like You to Know: Administrative Staff." **Public School Montessorian**. Vol. 3, No. 4, Summer, 1991.

Leonard, Gerry. "The Idea of the Erdkinder." **The NAMTA Journal**. Vol. 16, No. 3, 1991.

Lillard, Angeline Stoll. **Montessori: The Science behind the Genius**. New York: Oxford University Press, 2005.

Lillard, Paula Polk. **Montessori: A Modern Approach**. New York: Schocken Books, 1972.

Lillard, Paula Polk. **Montessori Today**. New York: Schocken Books, 1996.

Loeffler, Margaret (Ed.) **Montessori in Contemporary American Culture**. Portsmouth, NH: Heinemann Educational Publishers, 1992.

McNamara, John. "Elementary Montessori and Parent Education." **The NAMTA Journal**. Vol. 13, No. 1, Fall, 1987.

McTamaney, Catherine. **The Tao of Montessori: Reflections on Compassionate Teaching**. iUniverse.com, 2006.

Montessori, Maria. **The Child**. Adyar, India: The Theosophical Publishing House, 1941.

Montessori, Maria, **Reconstruction and Education**. Adyar, India: Theosophical Publishing House, 1942.

Montessori, Maria. **Peace and Education**. Madras, India: Vasanta Press, 1943.

Montessori, Maria. **Spontaneous Activity in Education**. New York: Schocken Books, 1965.

Montessori, Maria. **The Secret of Childhood**. New York: Ballentine Books Inc., 1966.

Montessori, Maria. **Dr. Montessori's Own Handbook**. New York: Capricorn Books, 1966.

Montessori, Maria. **The Absorbent Mind**. New York: Dell Publishing Co., 1967.

Montessori, Maria. **The Discovery of the Child**. New York: Ballentine Books Inc., 1967.

Montessori, Maria. **The Four Planes of Education**. Association Montessori Internationale Publication, reprint of lectures given in 1938 and 1939, edited by Mario Montessori Sr., 1971.

Montessori, Maria. **The Montessori Method**. New York: Schocken Books, 1972.

Montessori, Maria. **To Educate the Human Potential**. Madras, India: Kalakshetra Publications, 1973.

Montessori, Maria. **Education for a New World**. Madras, India: Kalakshetra Publications, 1974.

Montessori, Maria. **From Childhood to Adolescence**. New York: Schocken Books, 1976.

Montessori, Mario M. Jr. **Education for Human Development**. New York: Schocken Books, 1976.

Montessori, Mario M. Sr. **The Human Tendencies and Montessori Education**. Reprint of a lecture given in the Netherlands in 1956, Association Montessori Internationale, 1966.

Piaget, Jean. **To Understand Is to Invent: The Future of Education**. New York: Penguin Books (first published by UNESCO in 1948), 1976.

Rosen, Rae. "Junior High Lessons: The Voices of Experience in Middle School Programs." **Public School Montessorian**. Vol. 1, No. 4, Summer, 1989.

Schaefer, Lawrence. "A Montessori Vision of Adolescence." **The NAMTA Journal**. Vol. 12, No. 1, Fall-Winter, 1986.

St. Giermaine, Joyce. Ed. "The Montessori Farm School." **Tomorrow's Child**. Vol. 8, No. 5. Back to School 2000.

Standing, E. M. **Maria Montessori: Her Life and Work**. New York: Mentor Books, 1962.

Stephenson, Margaret E. "Adolescence—An Exploration." **AMI Communications**. Vol. 3 (from a lecture presented at the National Study Conference on the needs of Youth in the Third Plane of Development, held in Atlanta, Georgia, USA in April 1981) 1982.

Stephenson, Margaret E. "Montessori—An Unfolding—The Child from 3 to 6." **AMI Communications**. Vol. 1, No. 2., Copyright: Margaret E. Stephenson and AMI, 1971.

A Glossary
of Montessori Terms

Absorbent Mind. The mental capacity, especially of the young child, to take in information and sensations from the world.

Abstraction. The act of drawing conclusions, conceptualizing, generalizing, synthesizing or imagining from experience in the concrete world.

Auto-education. Self-teaching and self-learning through use of didactic materials, objects and activity.

Children's House. Translation of **Casa dei Bambini,** the name of the first Montessori program in Italy. Often used to refer to any Montessori program for preschool-aged children between the ages of two and six.

Control of Error. A feature or features of a learning material or activity which allows the learner to detect if mistakes or errors have been made. The control may be within the material itself, in the child and his or her memory or perceptions, or in the adult or another child.

Cosmic Education. A learning approach which offers a holistic view of human culture and knowledge and promotes an awareness of the connections among events and the interdependency among things and life forms.

Cultural Studies. The content or act of learning and education about all human knowledge and history. Includes the traditional subjects of science, history, geography, humanities and social studies that Montessorians work to present within an integrated curriculum.

Early Childhood. The period of human development between birth and age six.

Elementary. The period of human development and schooling between the ages of six and twelve.

Erdkinder. German term for "earth child." Refers to Montessori's concept of an adolescent educational program which typically includes a school farm.

Exercise. A defined activity or set of activities intended to be done with a learning material or set of materials. Usually includes direct and indirect objectives, points of interest, controls of error, variations and extensions.

Extensions. An extension involves using a familiar material to teach new, usually more complex or abstract, concepts or skills.

Fundamental Needs of Human Beings. Basic things upon which human survival and civilization depends. These include the five physical needs of clothing, nourishment, transportation, shelter and defense, and the four spiritual needs of religion or philosophy, culture, vanity or social acceptance and communication.

Great Lessons. A series of stories intended to provide an overview of the elementary curriculum and the impetus for research and further learning. These include: the Story of the Universe, The Coming of Life, The Coming of Humans, The Story of Communication in Signs and The Story of Numbers.

Ground Rules. Basic standards and limits for behavior established to facilitate social harmony in a learning environment.

Human Tendencies. Basic, motivating predispositions in people that guide behavior. These include exploration, orientation, order, communication, repetition, exactness, activity, manipulation, abstraction and perfection.

Independence. The quality or condition of self-reliance, free from needing others or being controlled by them.

Indirect Preparation. Secondary aims of exercises or activities that lead to future success in learning skills or that may not be readily apparent. For example, work with the knobbed cylinders, using the pincer grasp, indirectly prepares students for handwriting.

Interdependence. Mutual need or reliance among things, individuals or groups for survival, comfort, growth, fulfillment or happiness.

Isolation of Difficulty. The act of separating a particular skill or concept into a specific exercise to facilitate its mastery.

Language Arts. Speaking, listening, reading and writing.

Lesson. An educational event or series of events usually involving some direct instruction by a teacher.

Liberty. Freedom. Related to degree of choices in learning materials, movement and participation in learning activities and groups.

Logical Consequences. Results or repercussions of an individual's or group's behavior that are generally imposed from outside the individual or group but that are clearly and reasonably connected to that behavior in the mind of the individual or group.

Materials. Educational objects or sets of objects.

Mathematical Mind. The intellectual quality or mental capacity of human beings to organize and categorize impressions and experience.

Mathematics. The study of quantities, numerals and their operations: addition, subtraction, multiplication and division. Includes measurement and problem solving involving quantities and numerals.

Montessori Method. The systematic approach to education developed by Dr. Maria Montessori.

Montessori Movement. The series of events, actions, plans and people tending towards the increased use and establishment of the Montessori Method.

Natural Consequences. Results or repercussions of an individual's or group's behavior that occur without interference from another individual, especially a teacher, parent or other care provider.

Normalization. The process of adjustment or adaptation resulting in an individual or group flourishing, thriving and being capable of independence and concentrated learning.

Peer Teaching. The act of working and learning together by students in an educational setting.

Planes of Development. Four stages of human growth that go from birth to maturity. These levels have distinct tasks and ideal conditions for learning and include Early Childhood, Elementary, Adolescence and Maturity.

Points of Interest. Features of a material or exercise that are likely to attract the learner's attention.

Practical Life. A curriculum area including materials, lessons, exercises, skills and activities involved in daily living and the care of the person, environment, plants, animals and social relationships of day-to-day existence.

Prepared Environment. The learning space designed and maintained by a Montessorian for the purpose of educating others.

Presentation. A demonstration of the use of material or set of materials.

Self-teaching. Act or acts involved in an individual educating him or herself.

Sensitive Periods. Specific times of intense interest in particular activities or for the learning of particular skills or concepts.

Sensorial. A curriculum area including materials, lessons, exercises, skills and activities involved in developing skills of perception and the mind's capacity to organize those perceptions in meaningful ways.

Silence Game. A learning activity designed to help children develop self-discipline, usually done in a group, in which learners sit still and strive to make no sounds.

Spiritual Development. The act of refining or bringing out the full potentialities and capacities of the human psyche, intelligence, emotion and will.

Spontaneous Activity. Self-initiated involvement or engagement in work or learning.

Three-Period Lesson. A systematic instructional procedure involving three distinct stages: 1. the association of a sense perception or experience with a term or concept, 2. recognition of the phenomenon corresponding to the term, and 3. memory and identification of the term or corresponding phenomenon to experience or perception.

Variations. Additional uses for materials or lessons, usually another way to teach the same concept or skill.